365 Spaces of the Americas

Fernando Luiz Lara

Lara, Fernando Luiz (author)

365 Spaces of the Americas, 2025,

367pp.

Design by Natalie Cheng
Philadelphia: Nhamerica Press, 2025.

ISBN: **978-1-946070-49-4**

1. The Americas.
2. Art.
3. American Spaces.
4. American History

Author's Note

In 2018 I decided to draw one space of the Americas every day and post it on social media platforms. The idea came from the realization that we don't know our own spatial history. Drawing one space everyday helped me investigate our history and I learned a lot in the process working on spaces that I had never heard about before and that is the root of the problem, our history has been erased, kept invisible. I hope these drawings prompt you to learn more, as they did to me.

Fernando Lara, Philadelphia, June 2025

January 1
The Idea

We have barely started to learn the spatial history of our own continent.

January 2
Teotihuacan

Could we understand Teotihuacan as an early form of equal society as proposed by Graeber and Wengrow in 'The Dawn of Everything'?

January 3
Kancha

Kancha is probably the best known Quechua word, as all soccer lovers know important enclosed public space!

January 4
Xingu

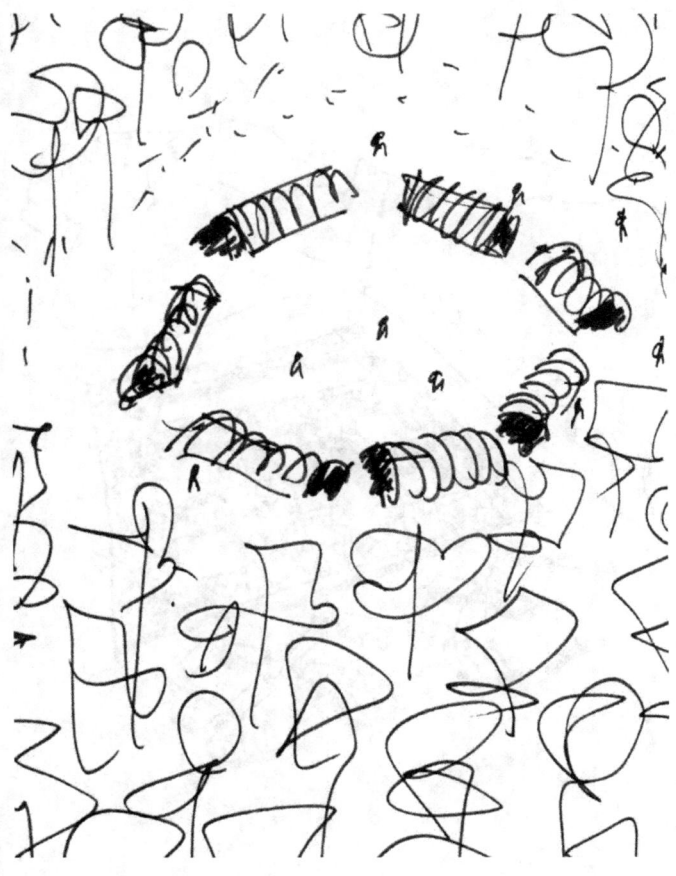

The people of Xingu believe that humans were created from wooden logs of the kuarup tree.

January 5
La Venta

The main site of the Olmec civilization (500 BCE-600 CE). The southern part of the island was destroyed to build an oil refinary. What a good summary of our continent it is!

January 6
Mapuche

Mapuche means "people of the earth", and as our Chilean friends know well, we desperately need to learn from their example.

January 7
Zuni

Zuni comes from the Spanish mispelling Shi'wi, meaning, "the flesh."

January 8
Carib

Caribs were originally Arawaks from the Amazon that became skilled navigators and warlords of the islands named after them: Caribbean.

January 9
Nazca

People have walked these paths for 2000 years, paying respect to the creation forces of the universe and keeping the lines alive simply by dislocating dust at every step.

January 10
Fig Island

As early as 5000 years ago, the first inhabitants of the Americas built shell rings on the coast of today's South Carolina.

January 11
Paracas

One of the mother cultures of the Andes, the Paracas, were weaving complex patterns 10,000 years ago.

January 12
Tupinambá

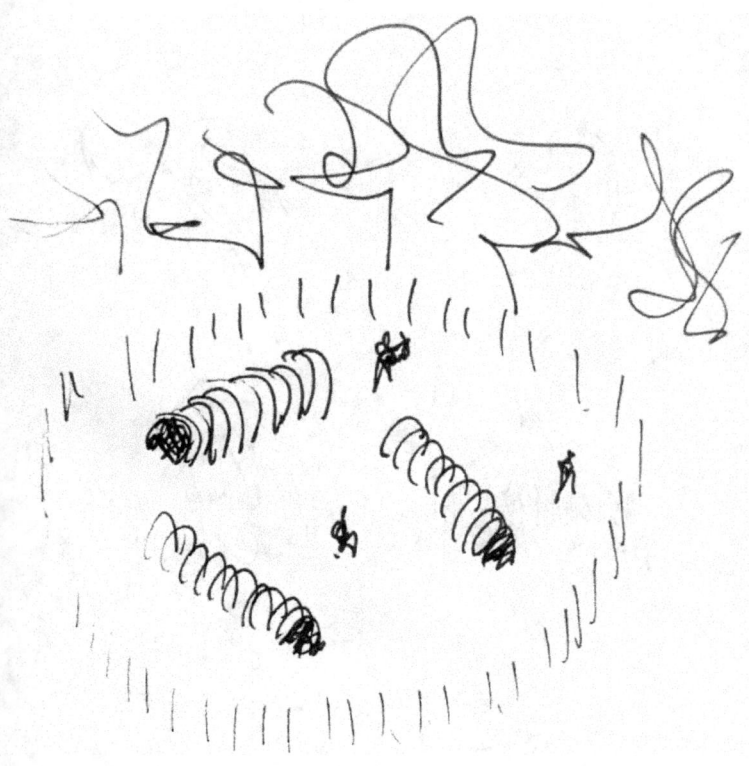

The first people to face the Portuguese in Bahia. From the Tupinambá came the first recorded critique of European culture, as registered by Montaigne in the 1570s.

January 13
Potiguara

In the northeast coast of Brazil, the Potiguara resisted for one full century, accepting an alliance with the Portuguese only in 1599.

January 14
Inuit

Around the year 1000 of our era, descendents of the Thule settled in the northern latitudes of our continent. They call themselves Inuit.

January 15
Caral

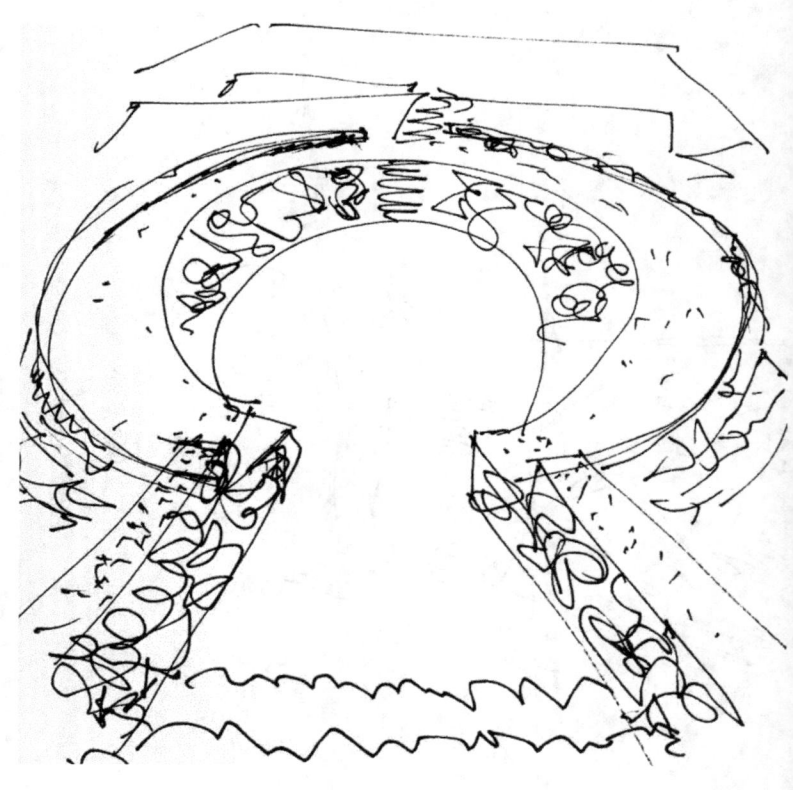

Considered the first city of the Americas, Caral was built 5000 years ago in the Pacific coast of South America. A complex society based on fishing, Caral shows no trace of warfare. Our first city was pacifist.

January 16
Sambaqui

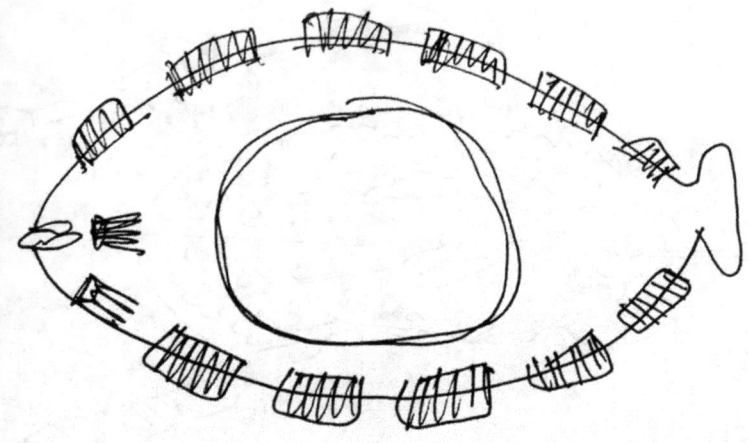

The earlier humans to inhabit the coast of Brazil, 8,000 years ago, built large mounds of shells that would calcify after years exposed to sun and rain. Think about domes built with slow-curing concrete.

January 17
Poverty Point

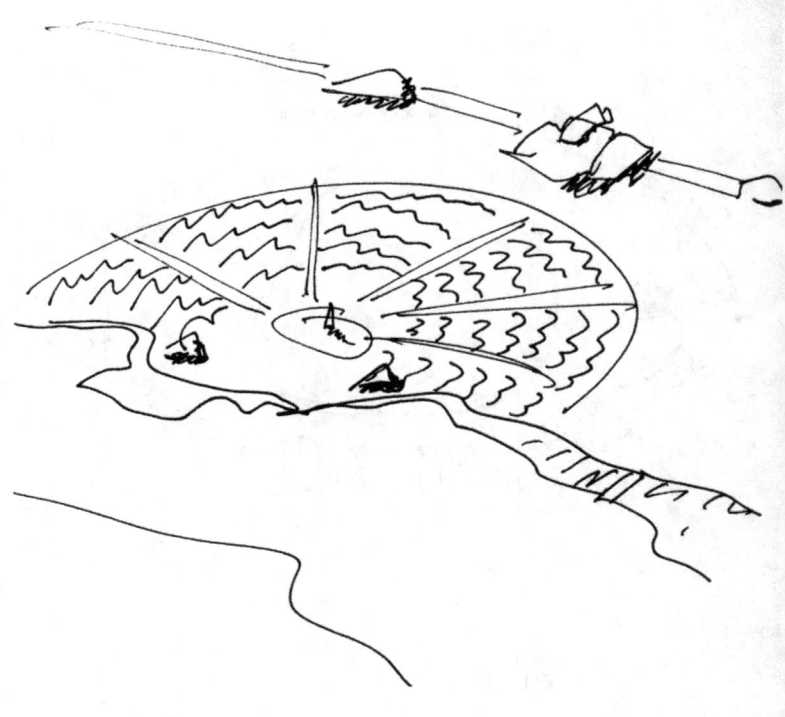

3,000 years ago the inhabitants of the lower Missisippi valley moved 2 million cubic meters of soil to create an artificial mountain along a large meeting plaza.

January 18
Sechin

Seschin is a granite hill carved with hundreds of anthropomorphic glyphs 4000 years ago. At its base is the oldest know builidng in the Americas, erected 3600 BCE.

January 19
Piraquê-Açu

From the Tupi: Pira means fish and Açu means big; the big fish of the Brazilian Atlantic coast, still inhabited by the Tupi-Guarani people.

January 20
Tolteca

In Nahuatl Toltec means cultured,
urbanite, the intellectual roots of
Pre-Columbian Mexico.

January 21
Yanomami

I learned from Hanna Limulja that Ya No Mami means "I am not dead."

January 22
Hohokan

Inhabiting the site of the contemporary city of Phoenix, the Hokokan built irrigation canals and rectangular pit houses.

January 23
Cueva de las manos

At 48 degrees south, where Patagonia meets the Andes, a group stencilled their hands in the walls of a cave, 13,000 years ago.

January 24
Cumbe Mayo

Cumbemayo means narrow river in Quechua, in reality an irrigation canal built 3500 years ago.

January 25
Meadowcroft

Located along the eastern banks of the Ohio river, Meadowcroft show signs of human habitation 19,000 years ago.

January 26
Pedra Furada

The rock paintings at Pedra Furada, Piauí, are only 12,000 years old, but charcoal and arrow shards are as old as 48,000 years, challenging the idea that humans came only from the Behring strait (Clovis hypothesis).

January 27
Monte Verde

The occupation of Monte Verde in the south of Chile (41 S) 18,000 years ago is another challenge to the Clovis hypothesis of human occupation solely via Siberia/Alaska.

January 28
San Agustin

In the lush valley of the Magdalena river in equatorial Andes, the people that inhabited San Agustin 2,000 years ago carved giant funerary statues in stone, inscribing their dead for eternity.

January 29
Guarany

One of the few languages to survive the European occution, Guarany is spoken by 7 million people today, mostly in Paraguay.

January 30
Cochiquinas

The Western foot of the Andes where the Amazon river grows has always been a center of equatorial civilization.

January 31
Aymara

The Aymaras believe that llamas brought water to the altiplano, and will return to the form of water springs at the end of time.

February 01
Tenochtitlan

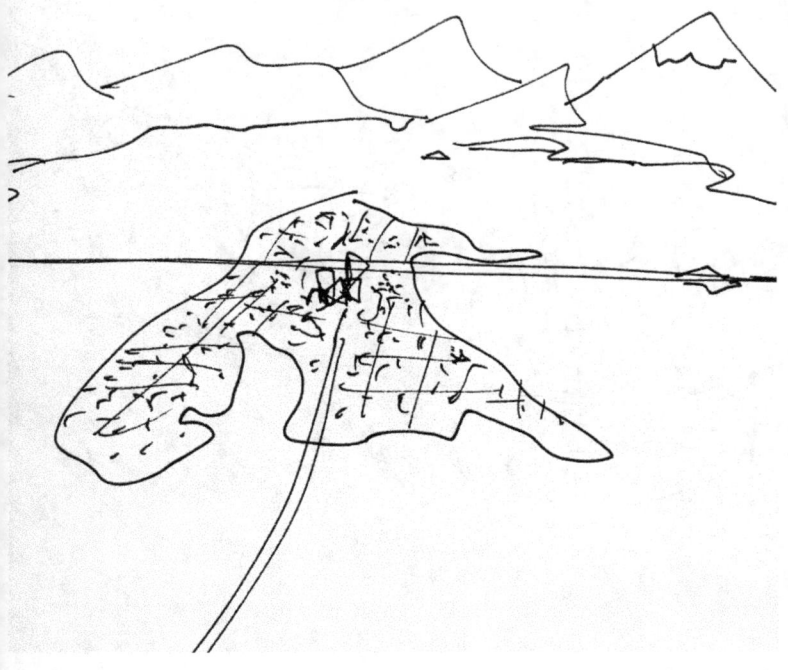

In a shallow lagoon the Aztecs founded their capital city, the largest ever in the Americas before 1500s, built along canals and chinampas - floating fields for cultivation.

February 02
Coricancha

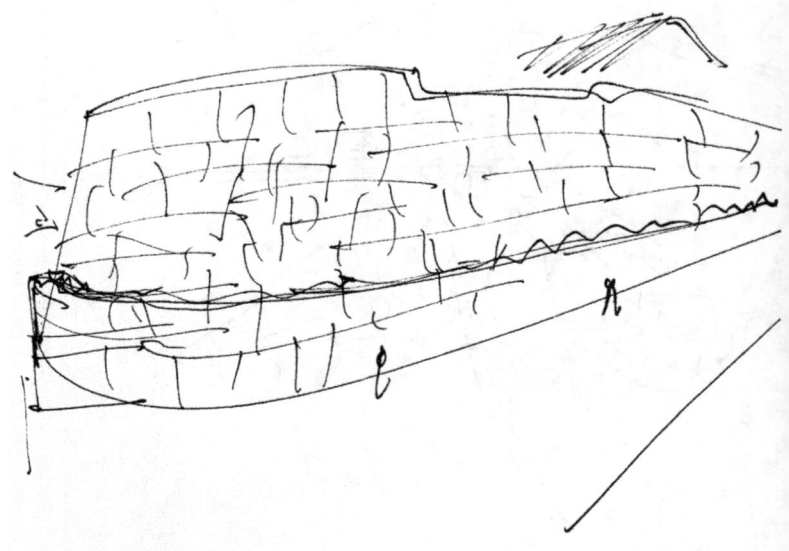

At the center of the Inka empire was the sun temple of Coricancha, at the center of today's southern empires are the socer fields, not coincidentally called canchas.

February 03
Tical

Tikal, or Yax Mutal - waterhole - in ancient Maya, was the center of the classic Mayan civilization 1800 years ago.

February 04
Kuhikugu

At the headwaters of the Xingu river in the Brazilian savana, the Kuikuro people built monuments to their gods along the terrain, horizontally.

February 05
Cañar

The great Cañari nation built
Ingapirca 4000 years ago.

February 06
Cantona

Cantona was a walled city of the Olmec-Xicalanca, built 1500 years ago.

February 07
Tumembamba 1493-1525

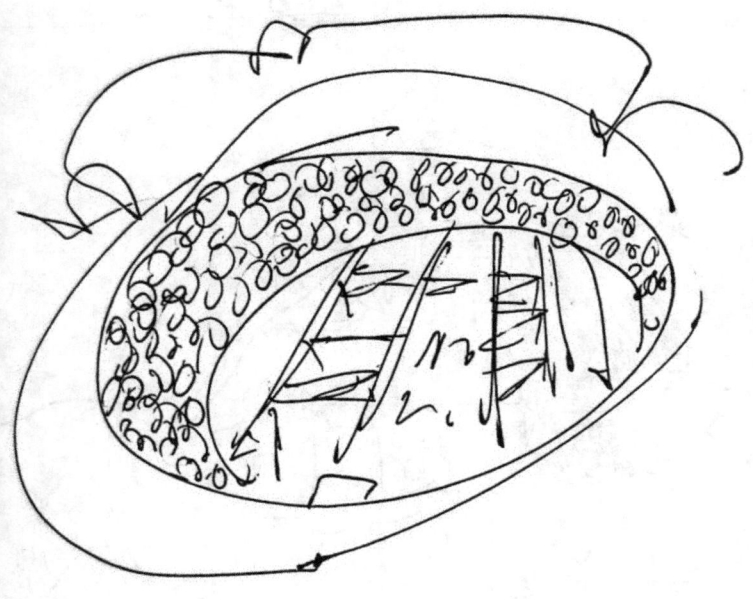

It is buried today under the contemporary city of Cuenca, Equador.

February 08
Corozal

Controlling trade between the Caribbean sea and the rivers Hondo and Nuevo, Corozal was an important Mayan settlement as early as 3,000 years ago.

February 09
Calakmul

In the Mayan lowlands of the Peten valley, Calakmul was the main city of the Kaan (snake) Kingdom, with 50,000 inhabitants around the year 800 CE.

February 10
Machu Pichu

Built as a palace for Pachacuti around the year 1450, Machu Picchu was so well hidden that no European was able to locate and sack the city for 450 years.

February 11
Huanuco Pampa

At three thousand six hundred meters (11,000 ft) above sea level, Huanuco Pampa was a gigantic celebration of the Inka bureaucracy, an architecture designed to convey imperial power.

February 12
Copan

In the year 837 of our era, the ruler of Copan, Uaxaclajuun Ub'aah K'awiil was assasinated, promtping a long period of instability that led to the abandonment of this great city some decades later.

February 13
Joya de Ceren

Around the year 600 CE, a large volcanic explosion covered the city with ashes, freezing Joya de Ceren as a unique window into the American past.

February 14
Tres Zapotes

Founded 3,000 years ago by the Olmec civilization, Tres Zapotes was continuously inhabited for over 20 centuries.

February 15
Cumbaya

The history of the Americas is written in stone.

February 16
Mesa Verde

For over 700 years the ancestral pueblo people inhabited the cliffs that today we call Mesa Verde.

February 17
Chan Chan

In a dry flat land quite close to the ocean, the Chimu people built an intricate network of canals that turned the desert into a fertile valley, with its capital, Chan Chan, the largest adobe city in the Americas.

February 18
Nadzcaan

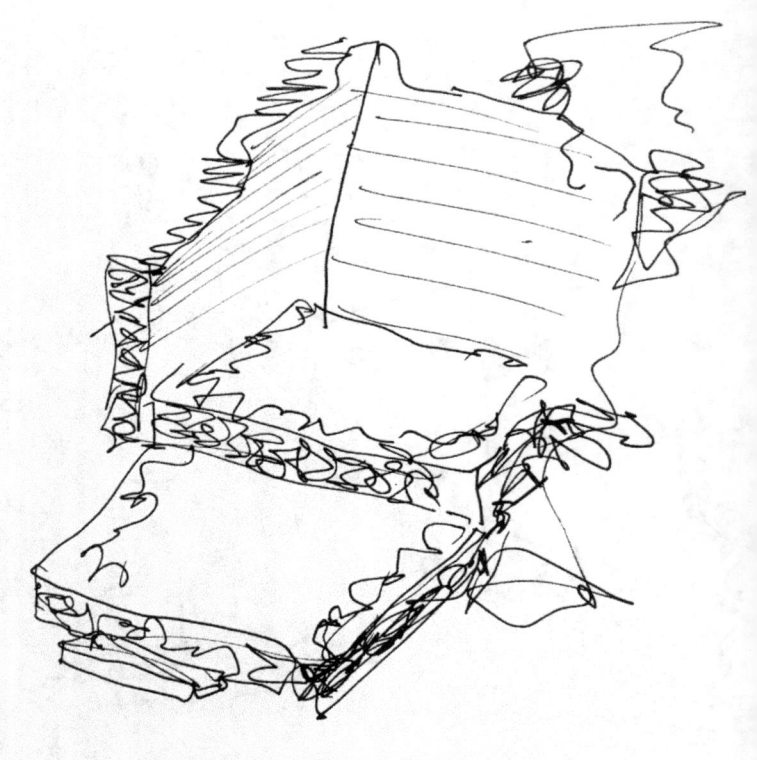

Close to the sky is the meaning of Nadzca'an in Mayan, a magnificent city unkown to European settlers until recently.

February 19
Angamuco

At the banks of lake Patzcuaro in Michoacan the Puerepecha bulit a large city that housed over 100,000 people 8 to 10 centuries ago.

February 20
Purus

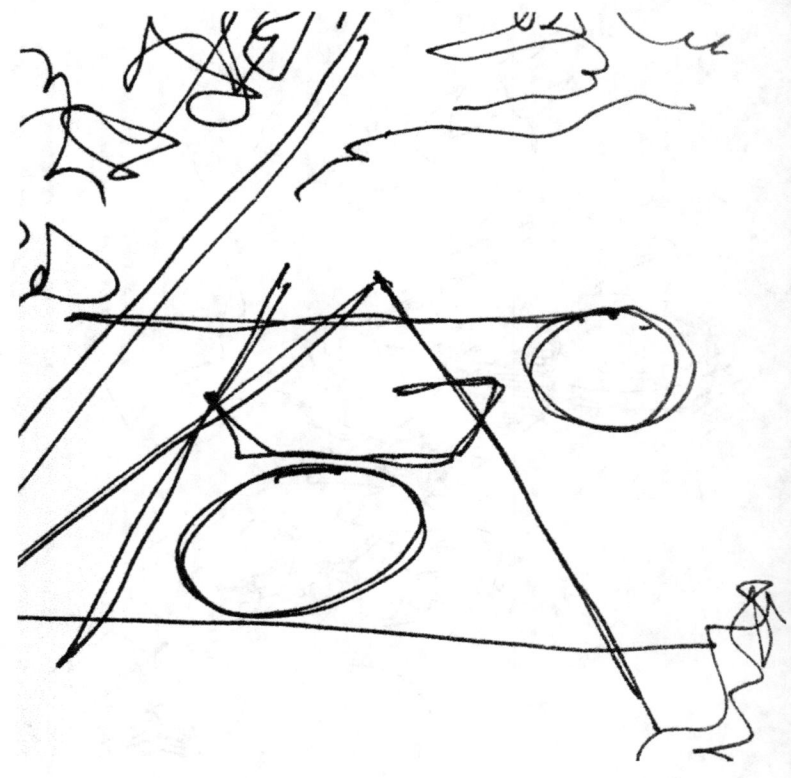

At the border of today's Brazil and Bolivia, the headwaters of the Purus river, the Amazonian inhabitants inscribed their socio-cosmologies in the earth.

February 21
Sayil

Twenty two centuries ago the Chontal people built the palace of Sayil.

February 22
Guanahatebey

The hunter-gatherers Guanahatebey inhabited the Greater Antilles before being displaced by the agriculturalist Taino.

February 23
El Pilar

Close to 180,000 Mayans inhabited the area of El Pilar (nowadays Belize) in the 10th century of our era.

February 24
Cahoquia

At the eastern banks of the Missisippi, right after it receives the water of the Missouri, was the urban complex of Cahoquia, the largest in the area that we today call The United States.

February 25
Uxmal

A magnificent complex in the Puuc style, Uxmal shows a level of craft and detail unmatched even by other amazing Mayan cities.

February 26
Xochicalco

Xochicalco—house of flowers—
in Nahuatl, was built by
Olmeca-Xicalanca that moved
west from the Campeche
region.

February 27
Chaco

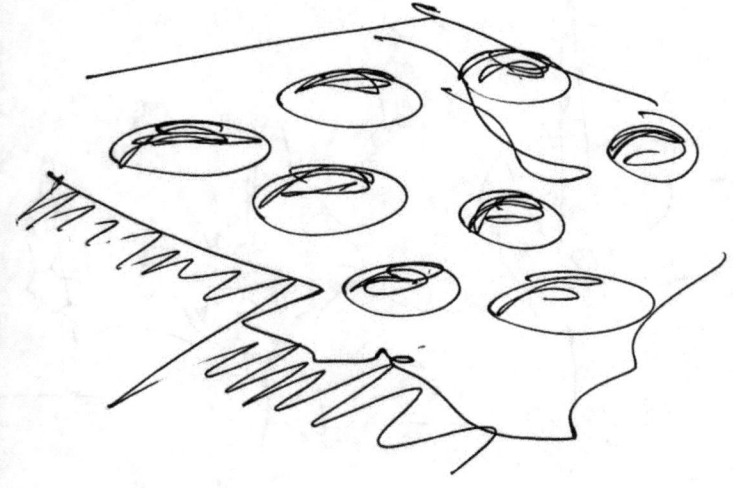

Chaco Canyon was the largest settlement of the ancient pueblo civilization around the year 1100 of our era.

February 28
Tastil

In the highlands of Atacama desert, the city of Tastil thrived until invaded by the Inka around the year 1500 of our era.

March 01
L'Anse aux Meadows

Ten centuries ago the Vikings tried to colonize the northeastern shores of America.

March 02
La Isabella

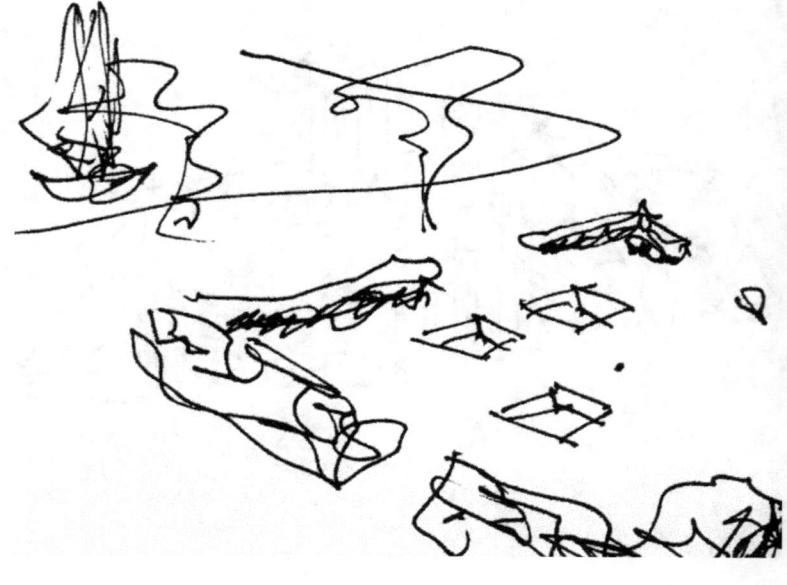

Founded by Columbus in 1493, La Isabella was the first city bulit by Europeans on the Caribbean islands.

March 03
Terra Nova de Bacalao

In 1476, 16 years before Columbus, the Portuguese navigator João Vaz Cortereal arrived in the island of Terranova, at the mouth of the Saint Lawrence river.

March 04
Santo Domingo

Founded on one side of the Ozama river in 1496 and connected to the other side in 1502, Santo Domingo is the oldest European city in the Americas still inhabited.

March 05
Marajó

The marajoara people inhabited this large island at the mouth of the Amazon river for 2000 years, until being almost completely exterminated by the European arrival in the 1600s.

March 06
Península de Paria

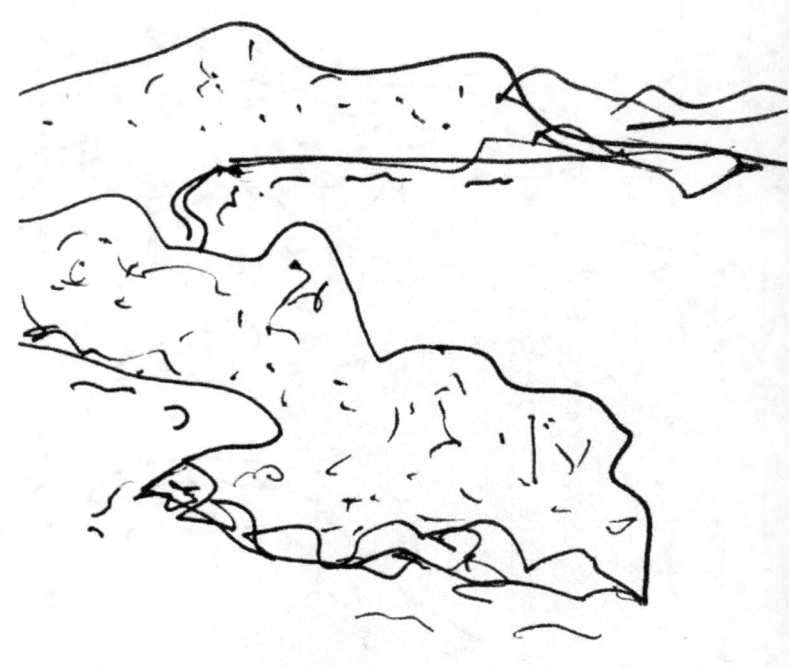

Columbus reached South America on his third voyage, landing in Paria in August of 1498.

March 07
Cabo Santo Agostinho

The spanish navigator Vicente Gomez landed in Cabo Santo Agostinho in january of 1500, four months before the Portuguese Alvarez Cabral who ended up claiming the land for his king.

March 08
Bahia de Todos os Santos

In 1501 the Portuguese had trouble choosing a saint for this large bay, called it Todos os Santos - all saints.

March 09
Las Tortugas

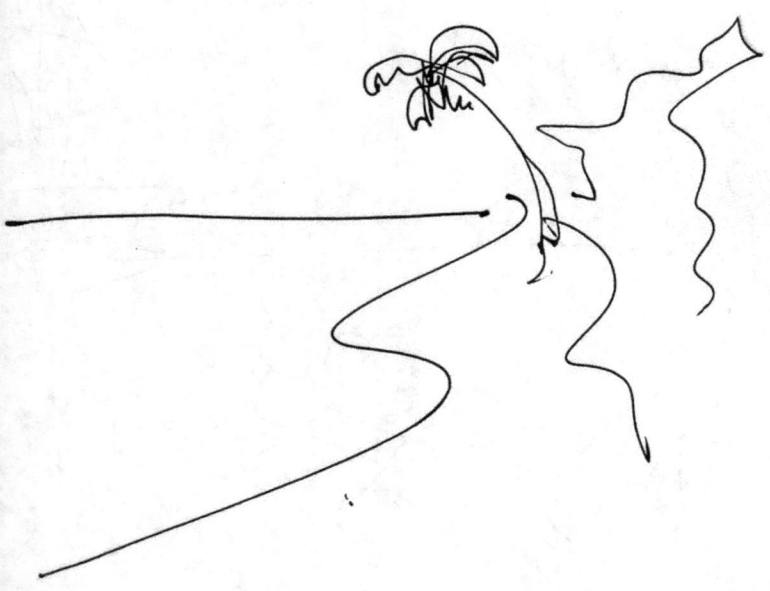

Directly north of La Habana and west of the Florida Keys are the three Tortuga Islands, a heaven for pirates.

March 10
Santa Cruz Cabrália

Named after the portuguese admiral Alvares Cabral and the holy cross of the European fanatics, is the land of the Pataxo who have resisted the Cruz for 523 years and counting.

March 11
Chakanputun

This chiefdom in the southern Yucatan peninsula was also called Can Pech, a name that survives in the present Mexican state of Campeche.

March 12
Caloosahatchee

The Calusa people had altered the Caloosahatchee river for centuries, buliding canals in the swamps to facilitate movement and trade.

March 13
San Juan

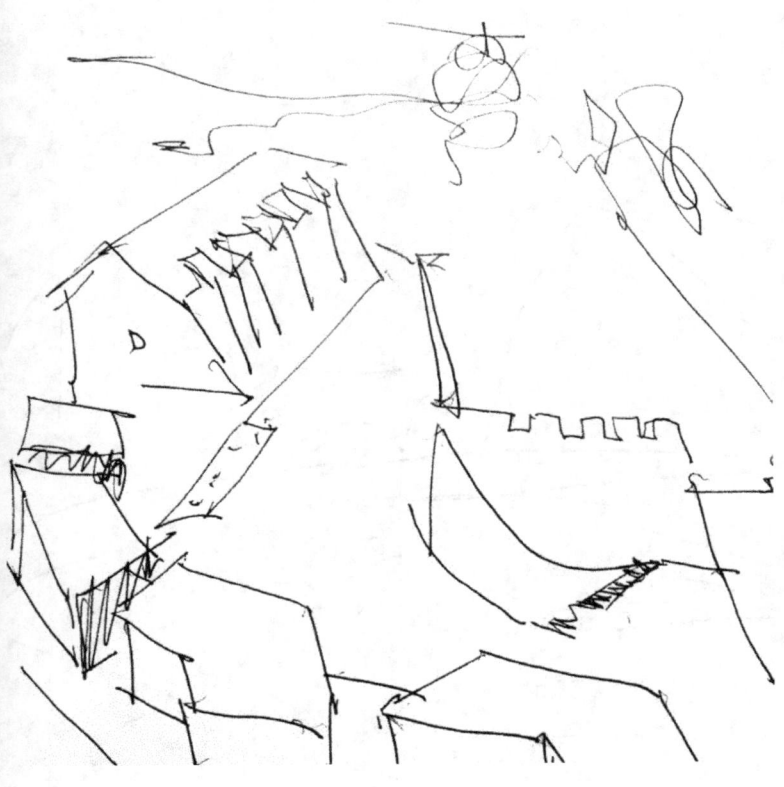

In the smallest but very strategic island of Puerto Rico, the Spanish built their city in 1521 and called it San Juan.

March 14
Guanabara

The bay where the Portuguese founded the city of São Sebastião do Rio de Janeiro was called Guaná-Pará (breast of the ocean) by its original Tupinambá inhabitants.

March 15
Catemaco

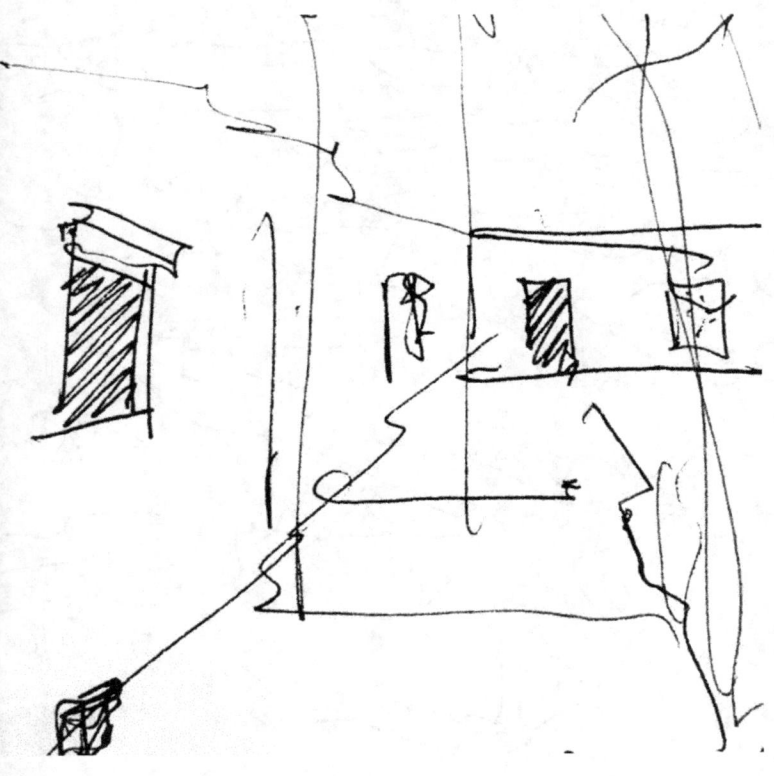

Founded by the Olmecs, Catemaco means "burned houses" in Nahuatl, perhaps due to a nearby volcano. Today the city is famous for its sorcerers.

March 16
Mississipi

The Obijawa words Michi Sepe mean the gathering of all waters.

March 17
Rio de la Plata

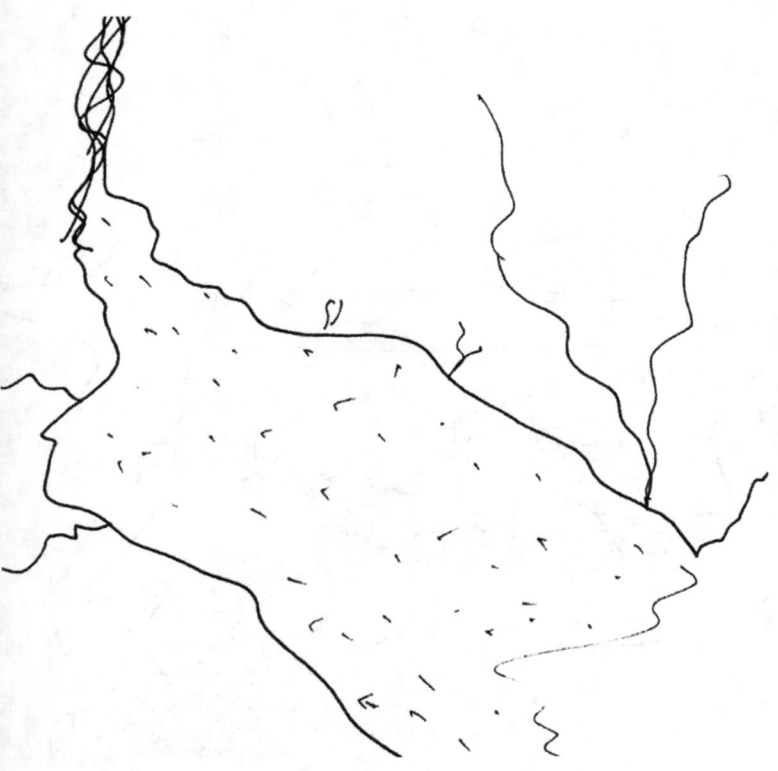

The silver (plata) was not at the large river formed by the Paraná and the Uruguay but 500 miles inland, in Potosi.

March 18
La Habana

The local Taíno leader was called Habaguanex, in the tradition of the Louisianas, Charlestons, and Bolivias we named after.

March 19
Santa Maria del Buen Ayre

Real de Nuestra Señora Santa María del Buen Ayre was founded once, destroyed by the local Charruas, and founded again 50 years later.

March 20
Iximche

Iximche was the main city of the Kaqchiquel, who initially allied with the Spanish invaders to raid other groups, but eventually grew tired of their demands and abandoned the place, burned by the desolate Castillanos.

March 21
Piaçabuçu

From large (gauss) palm tree (piaçava) in Tupi, the delta of the São Francisco river.

March 22
Santa Maria de Belém do Pará

In 1616 the Portuguese founded a city at the delta of the Amazon to control the river that looks like an ocean - Pa'ra in Tupi-Guarani.

March 23
Afuá

On the other side of the Marajó island the city of Afuá was built on stilts and is lucky to have no automobile access to this day.

March 24
Patagônia

From the vantage point of the iAndes, the kechua speaking people named the eastern lands Pata Ko - hilly lands.

March 25
Santa Maria del Darián

Founded by the Spanish in 1510, the city was destroyed by the Guna resistance and rediscovered only in the 21st century.

March 26
Cananéia

Settled in 1535, Cananéia sits right at the Tordesillhas line, the papal division of the planet between Spainish and Portuguese kingdoms.

March 27
Atacames

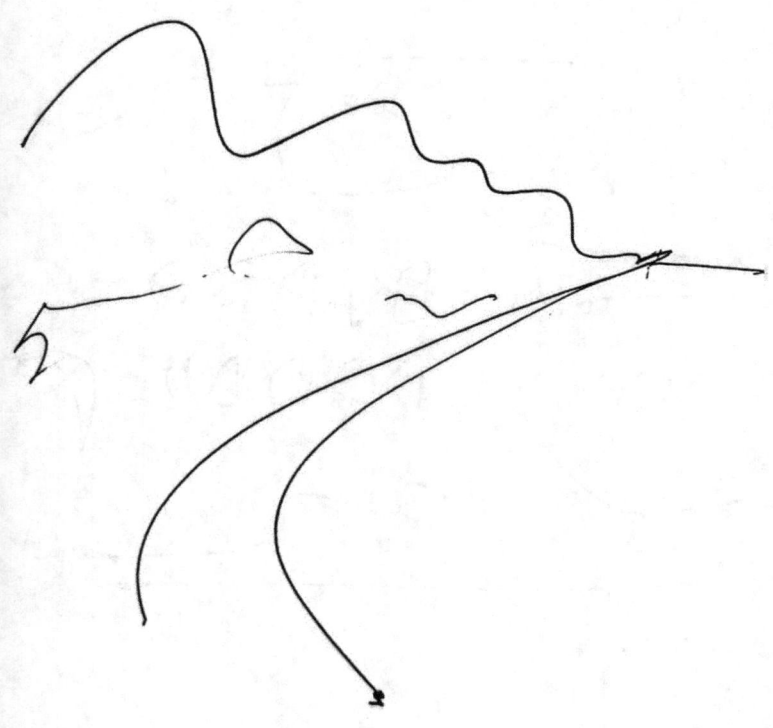

Africans who were able to escape their brutalized slavery created a settlement that is today's Atacames.

March 28
Cajamarca

Here Atahualpa was kidnapped by Pizarro and assassinated despite paying the ransom.

March 29
Punta Quemada

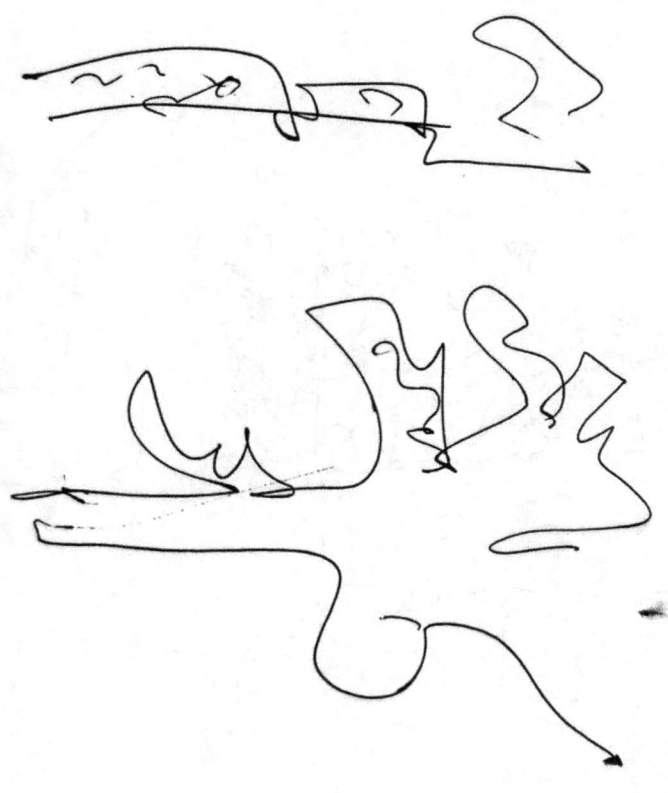

In 1525 Quitian warriors handed a heafty defeat to Pizarro's expedition at Punta Quemada (burned by the Spanish in their retreat).

March 30
Sacsayhuaman

The citatel of Sacsayhuaman, north of Cuzco, had its walls dismantled to build Spanish houses and temples in the main Inka city after 1532.

March 31
Metztitlan

Metztitlan was the center of the Otomi state, a group not conquered by the Aztecs at the time of the European invasion. Otomitl in Nahuatl means the ones who walk with arrows.

April 01

Millions died by bacterias and viruses drawn here to scale.

April 02
Cartagena

After the defeat of the local Karibs and the destruction of their village, the Spanish took control of the bay in 1533, making Cartagena a fundamental stop for all the riches of Mexico and Peru on their way to La Habana and Sevilla.

April 03
La Habana

The land of Habaguanex became another important knot in the thread that connected Mexico, Peru, Cuba and Sevilla.

April 04
Panama

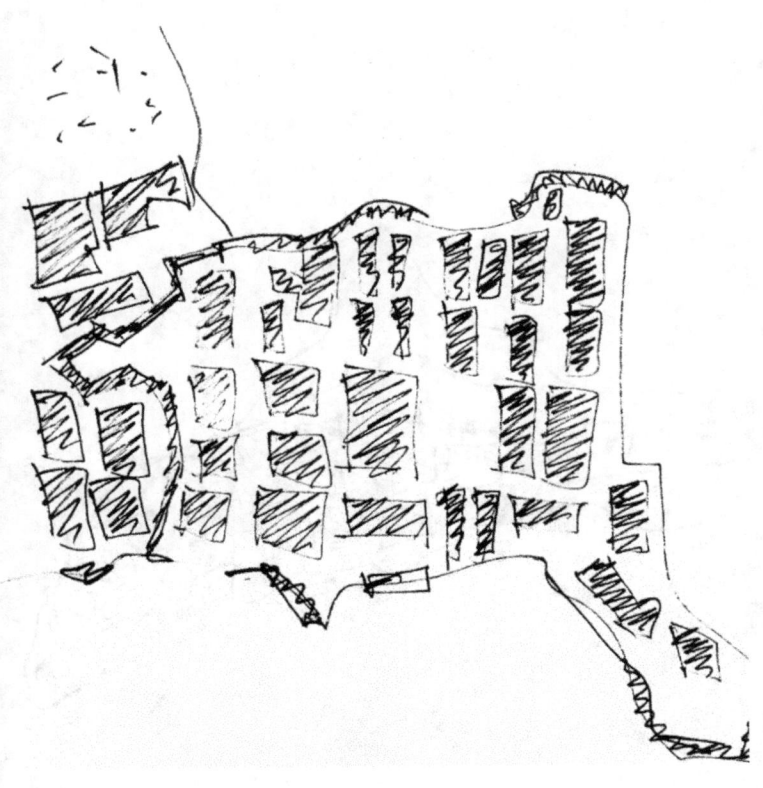

The Cueva and Cocle people called this place Panama after the abundance of fish.

April 05
San Juan

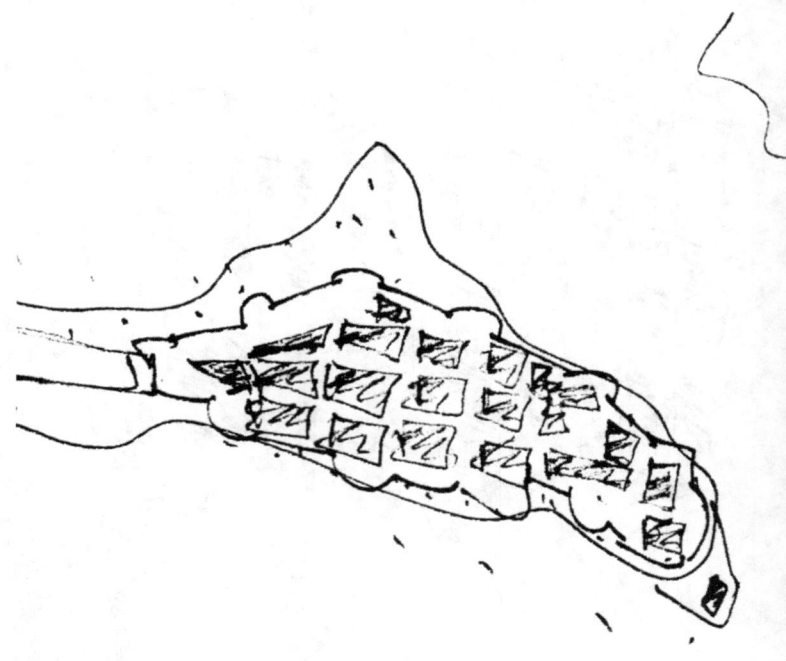

The old Ciudad de Puerto Rico was the third permanent settlement built by the Spanish invasors in the Americas, after Santo Domingo and Panama Viejo.

April 06
Santiago de Cuba

Built at the Southern end of the island, Santiago was the capital of the Spanish colony of Cuba from 1522 to 1589.

April 07
Santa Marta

Displacing the Tairona people, the Spanish built the city of Santa Marta.

April 08
Caracas

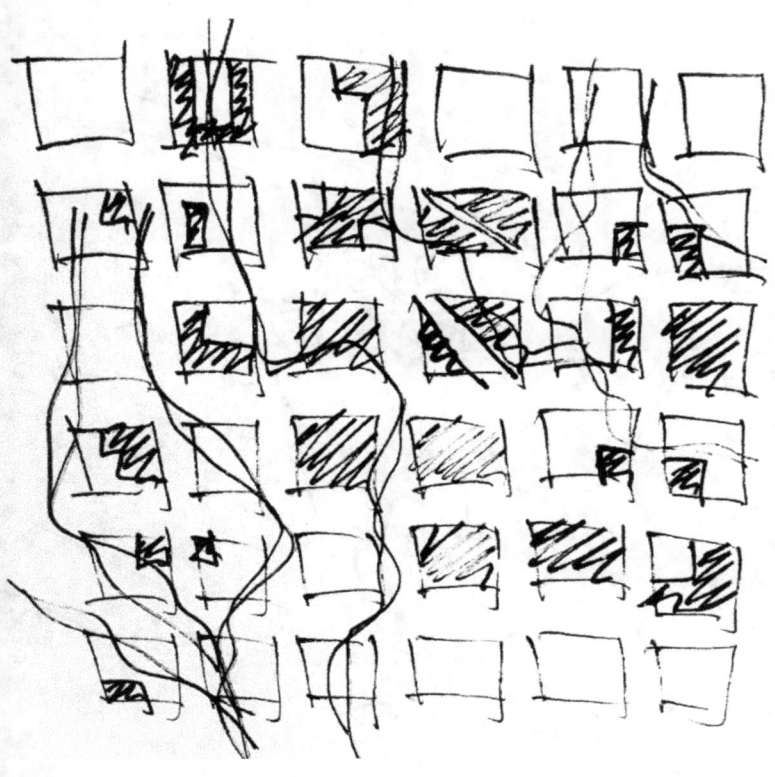

The Teques and the Caracas fought the Spanish invadors for a whole decade, until disease wiped them out and Diego de Lozada named his city after a catholic saint -Santiago - and the displaced inhabitants - Caracas.

April 09
San Agustin

The oldest European settlement in what is now the USA, Saint Agustine was founded by the Spanish in 1565.

April 10
Veracruz

When Hernan Cortez arrived at the Americas main land in 1519 he named the place after the cross he fanatically belived in.

April 11
Lima

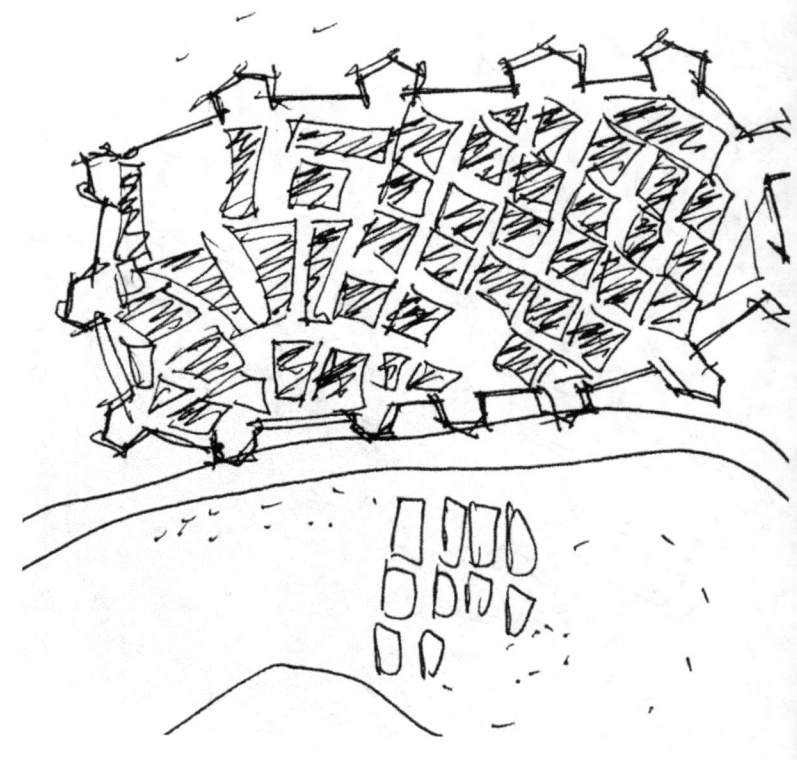

Named after an oracle - Lima means "the one who speaks" in Quechua - the site was renamed Ciudad de los Reyes by the Spanish invadors in 1535.

April 12
Potosi

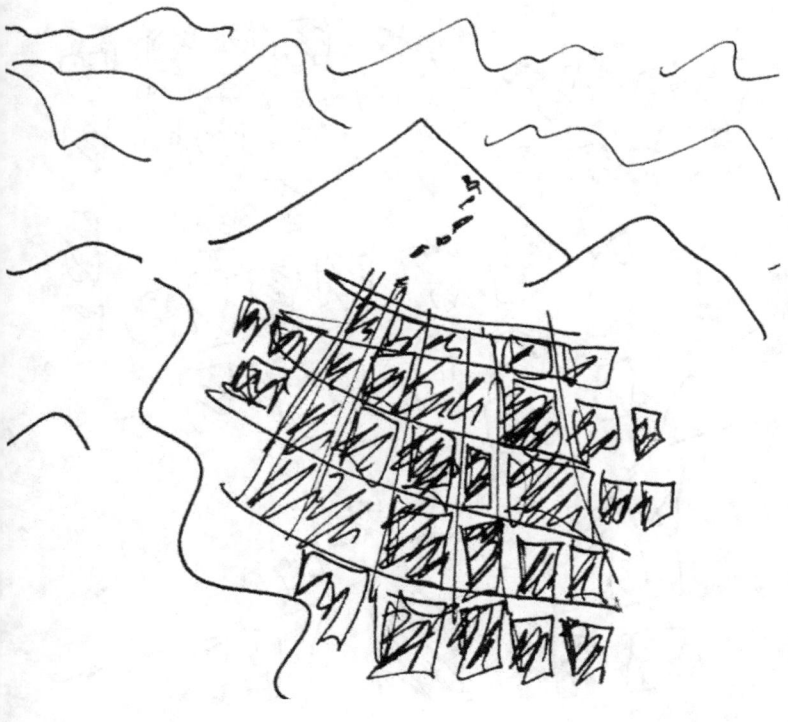

The exploitation of silver at the Serro Rico de Potosi forced thousands of local Aymara and Quechua people into a system of indentured servitude called mi'ta.

April 13
Guadalajara

The fierce resistance of the Caxcan, Portecuex and Zacateco groups forced the Spanish to abandon the old village of Guadalajara and create a new one in 1542.

April 14
São Paulo

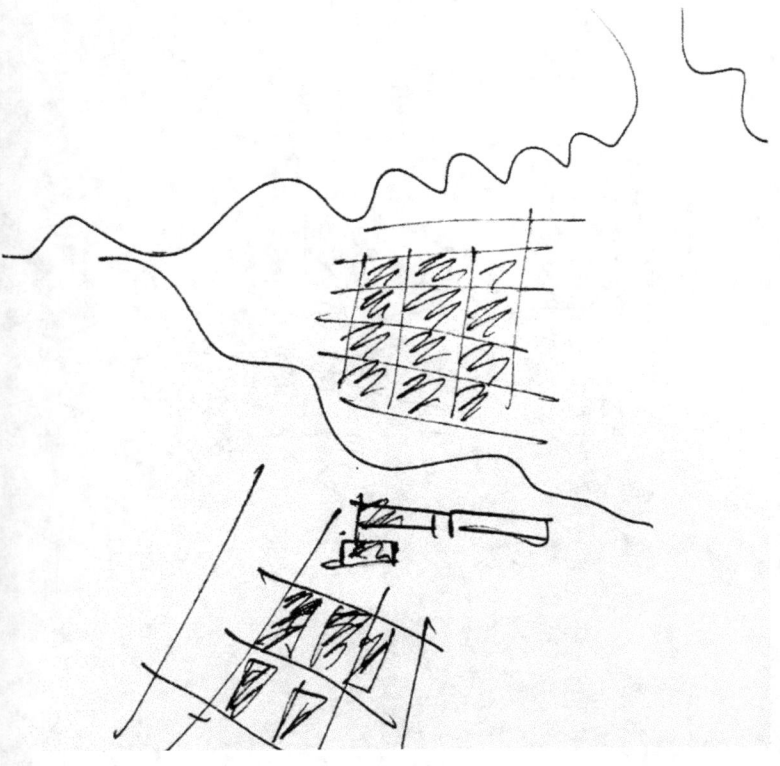

Jesuit priests founded a school - Colegio de Piratininga - in 1554, originating the city that they would later call São Paulo.

April 15
Salvador

To protect the Bay of All Saints, the Portuguese built a fort at the peninsula and named the settlement after 'the savior" - Salvador.

April 16
Philadelphia

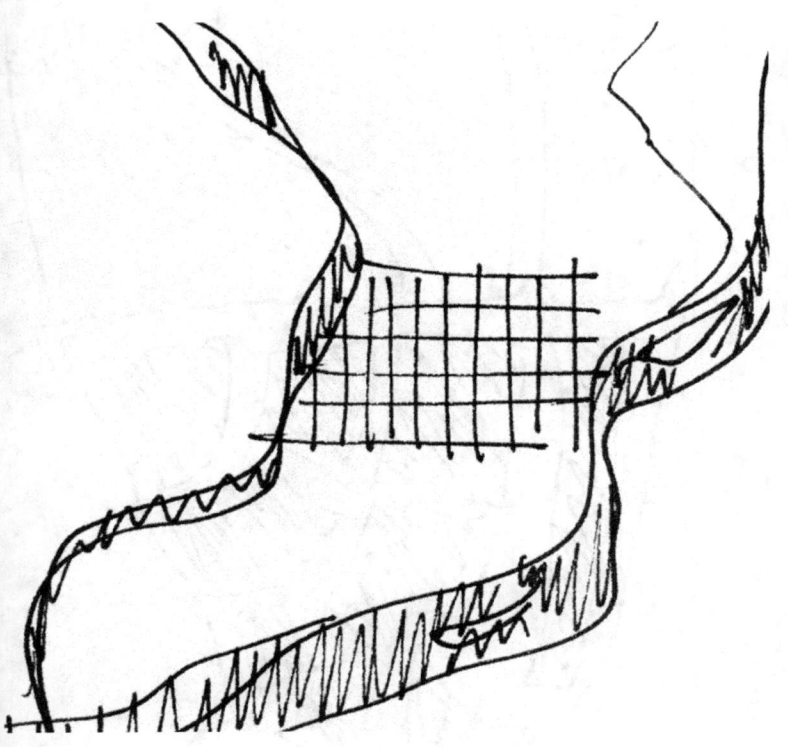

Founded by William Penn in 1682, the city of brotherly love would become the most important and the first capital of The United States of America in the 1770s.

April 17
New Amsterdam

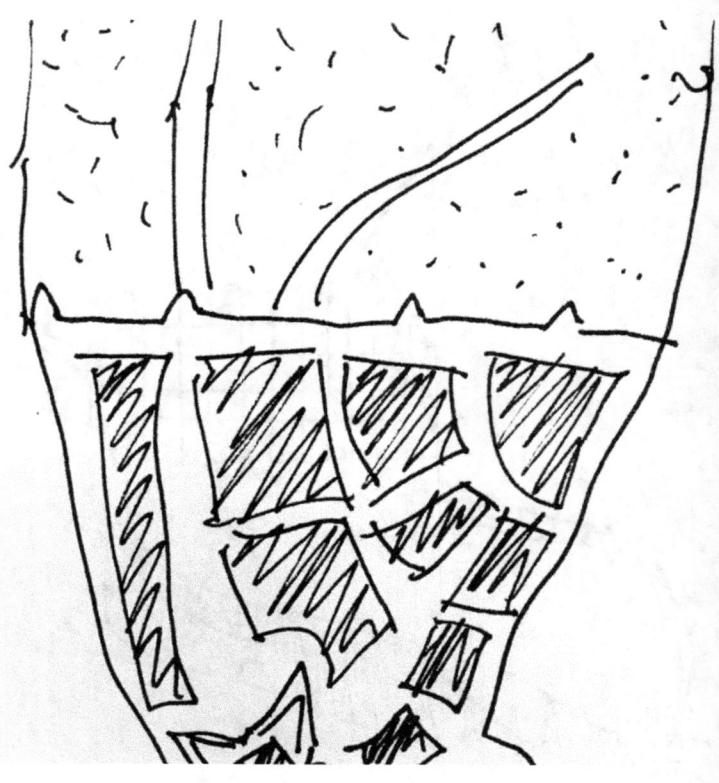

Named Manhattan by the native Lenape people, the island was renamed New Amsterdam by the Dutch invadors in 1625.

April 18
Santiago de Chile

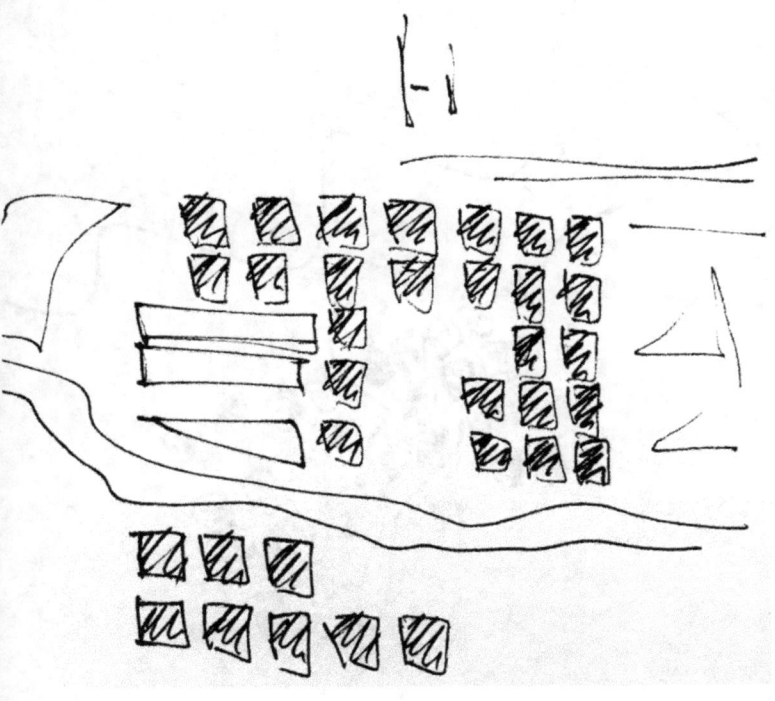

In 1541 Pedro de Valdivia entered the fertile vally of the Mapocho river, displaced the residents and founded the city of Santiago de la Nueva Extremadura.

April 19
Santa Fé de Bogotá

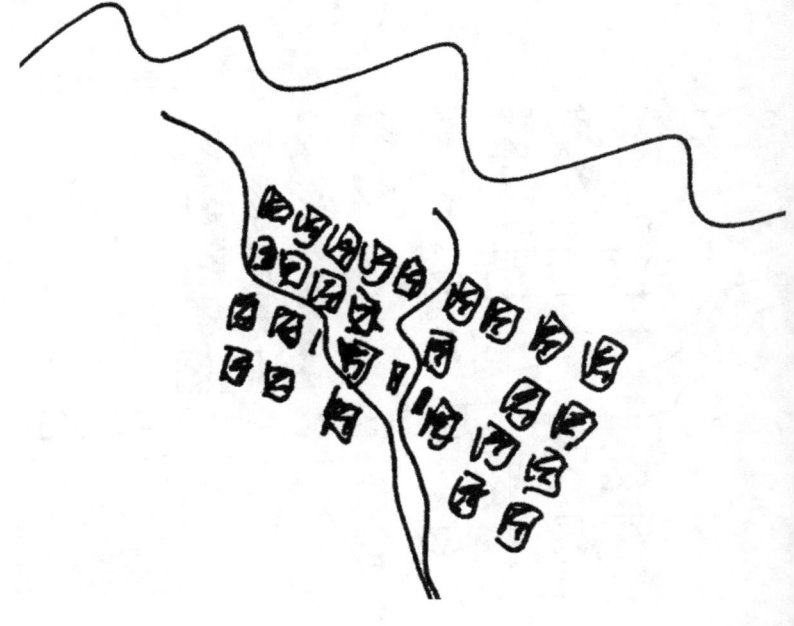

The Muiscas called this side of the hill Bacatá, a place invaded by Gonzalo de Quezada and renamed Santa Fe de Bogota.

April 20
Buenos Aires

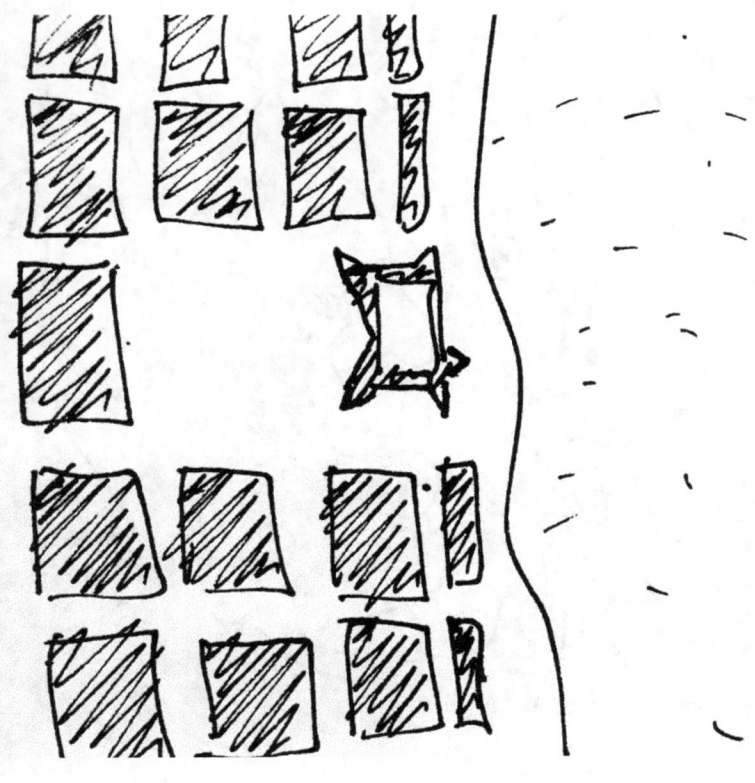

Buenos Aires was founded twice in the lands of the Tehuelche. The first invasion of 1541 was rebuked. The second invasion of 1580 gave the Spanish a fortification to control the river to acess Potosi - Rio de la Plata.

April 21
São Luis do Maranhão

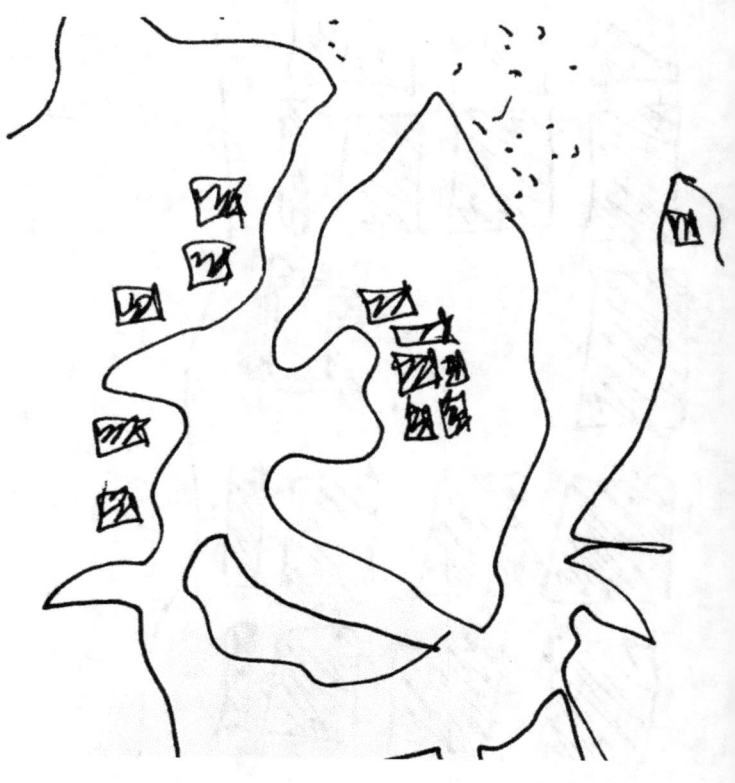

The french claimed the Tupinambá island of Upaon-Açu and named if after their King Luis.

April 22
Campeche

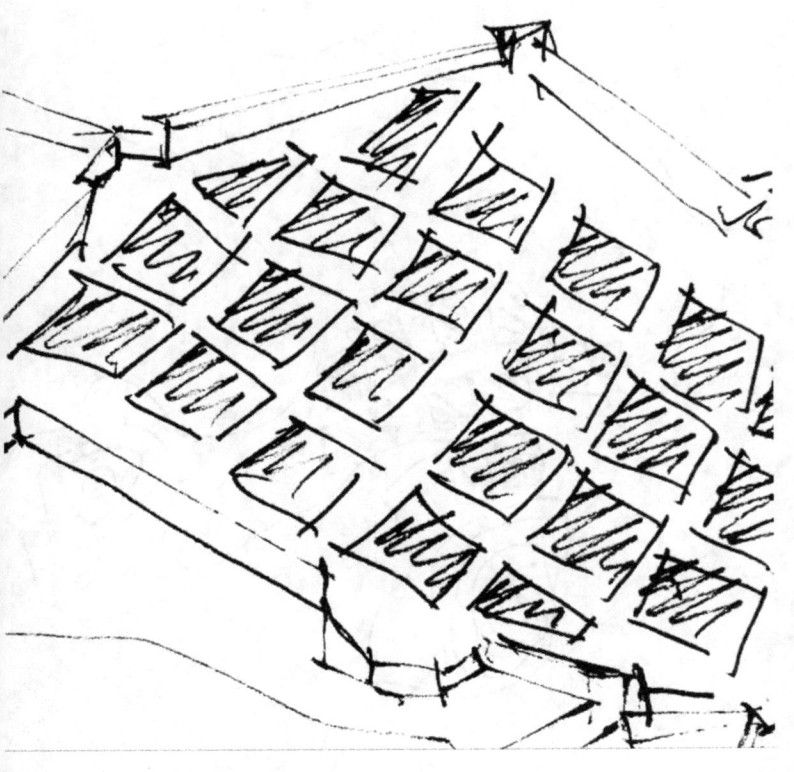

Can Pech was a Mayan city renamed Campeche by Francisco de Montejo in 1540.

April 23
Boston

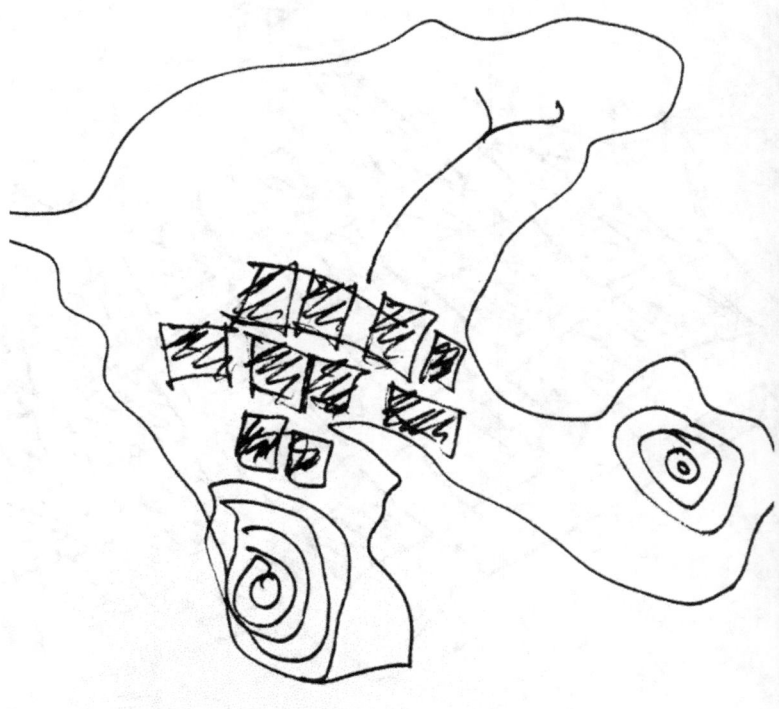

Massachusett was the name of the group that lived in the Shawmut peninsula before John Winthrop.

April 24
Antigua Guatemala

Founded in Iximche in 1524, it was moved to Almolonha in 1527 and to the valley of Panchoy in 1541, where it still sits.

April 25
Belém

Named initially as Feliz Lusitania (happy Portuguese), Belem sits over the Mairi lands.

April 26
Recife

In 1630 the Dutch took control of Olinda and, abandoning the hill, decided to occupy the sand banks (arrecifes) of the Capibaribe and Beberibe rivers.

April 27
Tampico

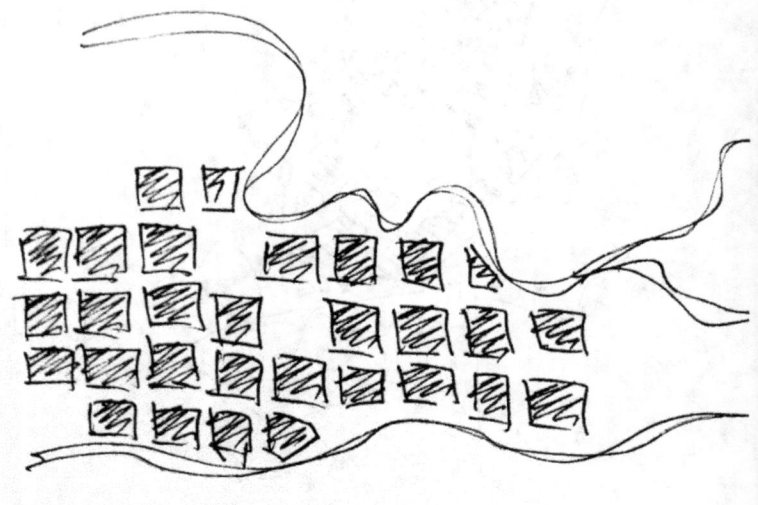

The "place of the dogs", in the Huasteca language, Tampico sits at the mouth of the Panuco river.

April 28
New Orleans

Called Balbancha or "place of many tongues." by the natives, New Orleans still holds the character of a cosmopolitan city.

April 29
Puebla

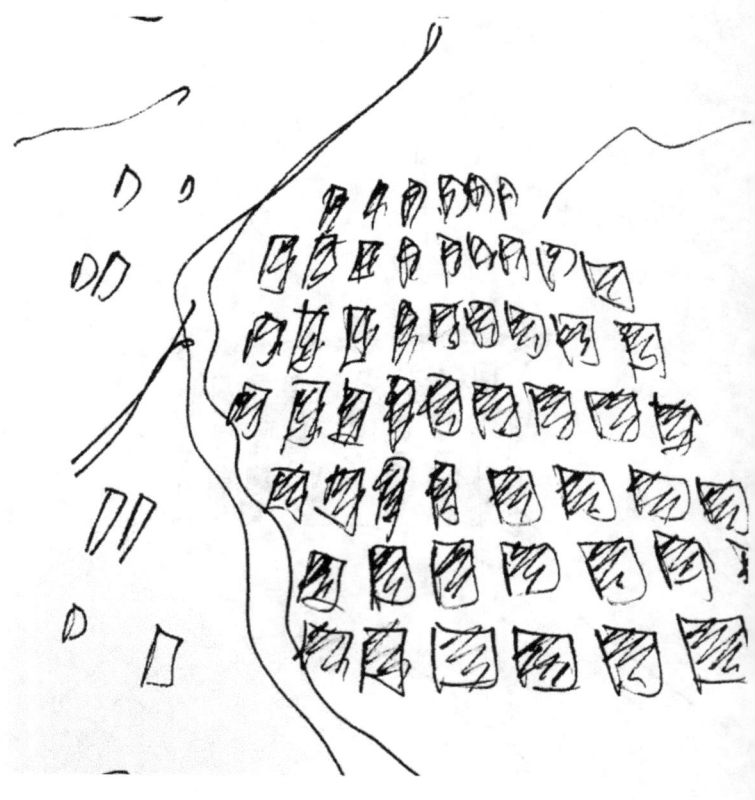

Allegedly founded on "empty" territory, the plan of Puebla is as much renaissance as it is a copy of the plan of Cholula, its indigenous neighbor.

April 30
Quebec

Stadacona was the Iroquois settlement where Quebec sits today.

May 01
Atlantic

Over 12 million people were enslaved and transported across the Atlantic to sustain the European invasion.

May 02

First African slaves brought by Juan de Cordova

Juan de Cordoba, originally from Seville, was the first merchant to get royal authorization to trade people between Africa and the Americas.

May 03
Agriculture

One of the main justifications for European land grabbing was the absence of "agriculture" defined as the removal of all life for a single species to grow.

May 04
Industry

Indigenous bodies, from here or from Africa, have always been the main power of all industries in the Americas.

May 05
Transportation

African bodies were the transportation system of the Americas.

May 06
Domestic work

Indigenous female bodies, from here or from Africa, did all domestic work for the Europeans and their descendants.

May 07
Salvador

From 1530 to 1830, Salvador recieved 1,214,036 enslaved Africans.

May 08
Cartagena

The Sinu lived in a village caleld Calamarí which was abandoned before the arrival of conquistador Pedro de Heredia.

May 09
Veracruz

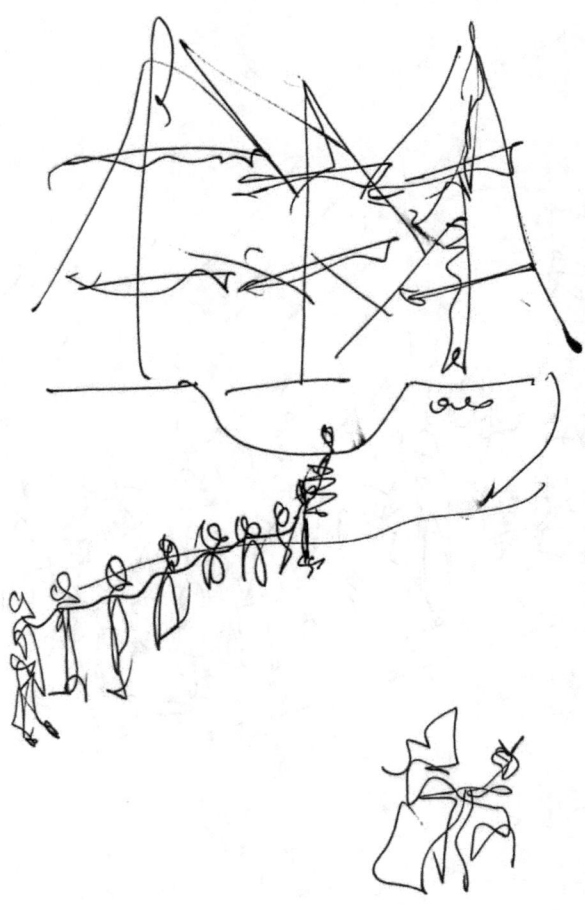

When Hernan Cortez arrived in the American mainland in 1519 he named the place after the cross he fanatically belived in.

May 10
Sapelo Island 1526

Occupied by Spanish missionaries since the 16th century, Sapelo Island is now home to the Gullah Geechee, descendants of the first Africans enslaved in the Carolinas.

May 11
Serra da Barriga/Palmares 1605

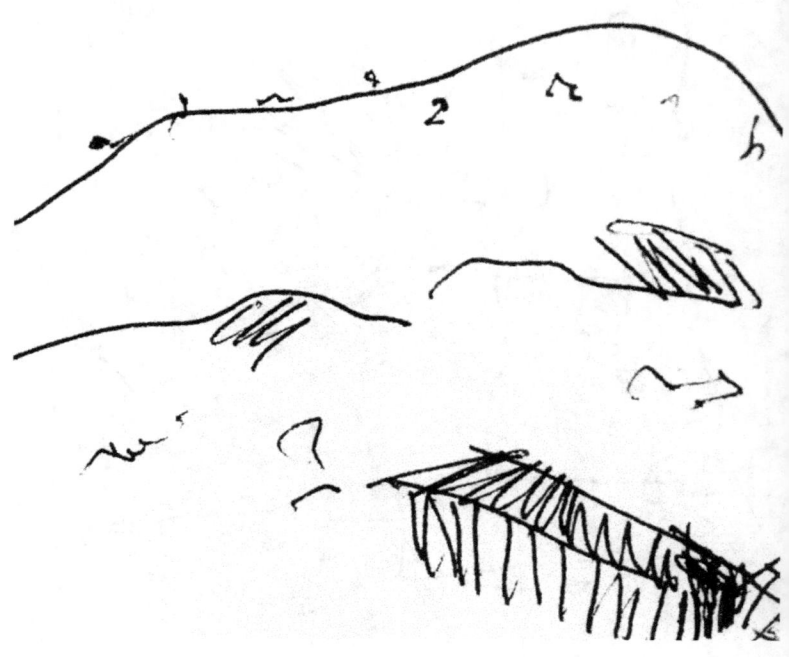

For almost a century (1605-1694) the free black territory of Palmares resisted both Dutch and Portuguese attacks in the Brazilian Northeast.

May 12
San Lorenzo de los Negros

Led by Gaspar Yanga, San Lorenzo de los Negros first fought the Spanish in 1609 then negotiated territorial autonomy in 1618.

May 13
Santa Ana de Coro

In 1795 the Santa Ana de Coro rebellion, led by Jose Chirino, attempted to end slavery and white supremacy.

May 14
Curaçao

Also in 1795 the Curaçao rebellion, led by Tul'a, attempted to end slavery and white supremacy.

May 15
Granada 1795

And still in 1795 the Granada rebellion, led by land owner Julien Fedon, attempted to become independent from British rule.

May 16
Engenho Santana 1789

The Engenho Santana rebellion was not exactly for abolition of slavery but for regulating work conditions: one day of rest, no whip, better food.

May 17
Stono River 1739

The largest slave rebellion in North America was the Stono River revolt of 1739.

May 18
New York 1741

In 1741 Manhattan had the second largest enslaved population in British North America, and a series of arsons were bundled together as slave revolt.

May 19
Prosser plantation 1800

The Prosser plantation revolt of 1800 was led by Gabriel in the young state of Virginia.

May 20
Coromantee 1760(1605)

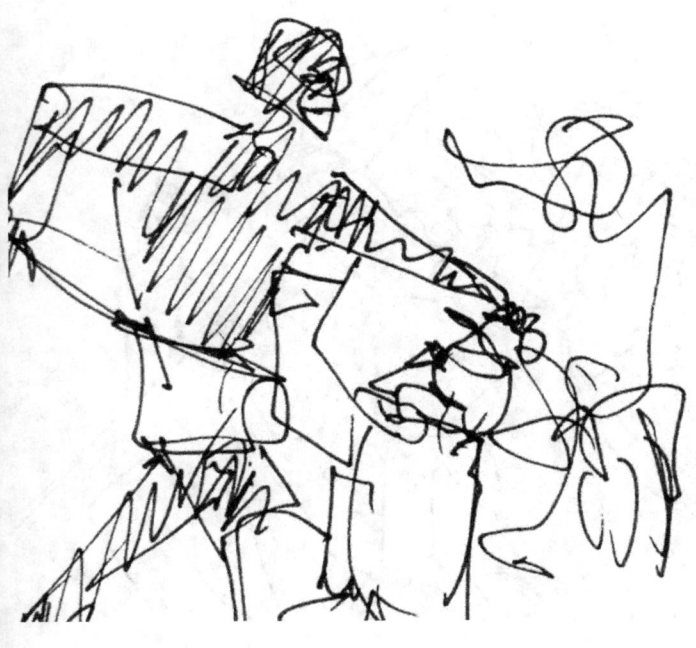

The Akans, also known as Coromantees, led several revolts in the American colonies: Antigua, New York, Virgin Islands and Jamaica.

May 21
Salvador 1835

The Malês, being literate in arabic, plotted a revolt that paralized the city of Salvador in 1835.

May 22
Triunvirato 1843

Carlota Lucumi was a yoruba woman who led the revolt in the Triunvirato plantation, in the island of Cuba, in 1843.

May 23
Haiti 1804

The first and only succesful slave revolt in the Americas was fought from 1791 to 1804 and resulted in Haiti declared as a black republic.

May 24
Charleston 1822

Denmark Vesey planned a revolt in Charleston to coincide with the bastille day of July 14th 1822, but was betrayed a few weeks before and executed on July 2nd.

May 25
Virginia 1831

Net Turner led the Virginia revolt of 1831, the deadliest in US history.

May 26
Demenara 1823

Ten thuousand enslaved people rebelled in Demenara, Guiana, in 1823.

May 27
Aponte 1812

Led by Jose Antonio Aponte, cubans in Camagüey and Bayano attempted a revolt to end slavery.

May 28
Hausa

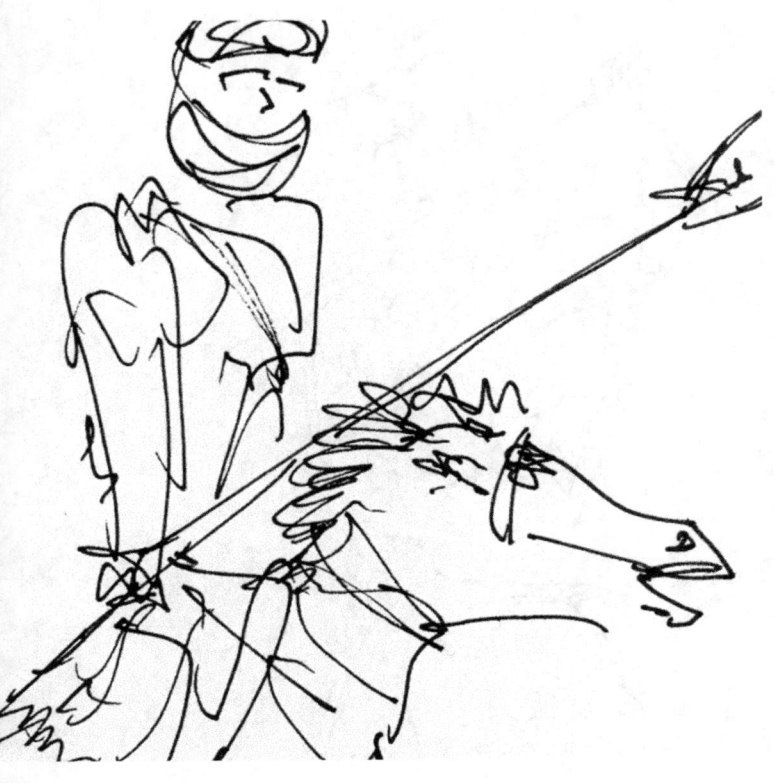

Before the big revolt of 1835, the Malês, also known as Hausa, had rebelled in 1807.

May 29
Guamacaro 1829

The revolt of the enslaved in Guamacaro, 1825, is special because the land owners were from the young republic of the USA.

May 30
Vallano

In Vallano (or Bayano) Panama there were so many revolts they called it a war.

May 31
Jamaica 1728

Jamaican Maroons rebelled against the British in 1728 and held the rebellion for a whole decade.

June 01
Monclova 1607

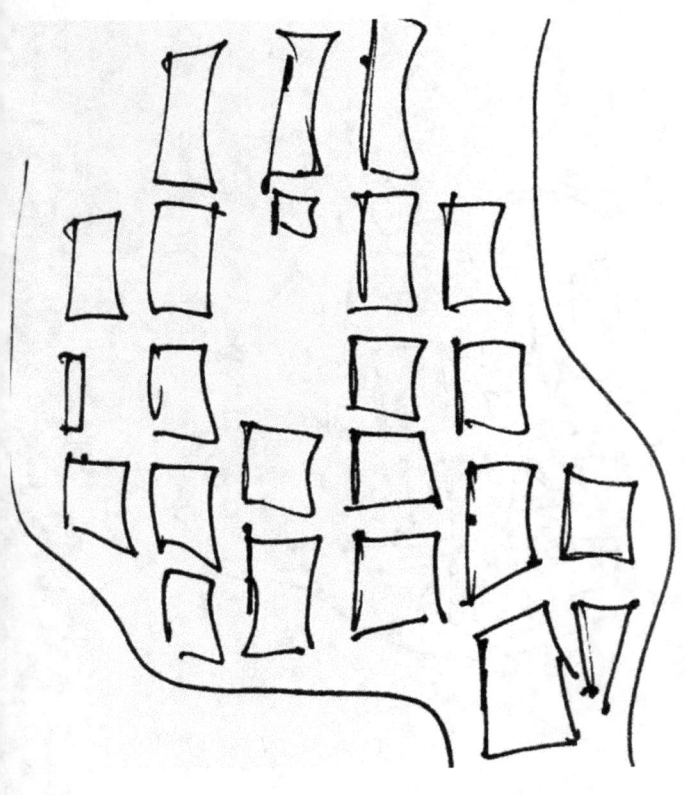

Monclova, just south of the Rio Grande's big band, would later be the capital of Coahuila y Tejas.

June 02
Santa Fe 1608

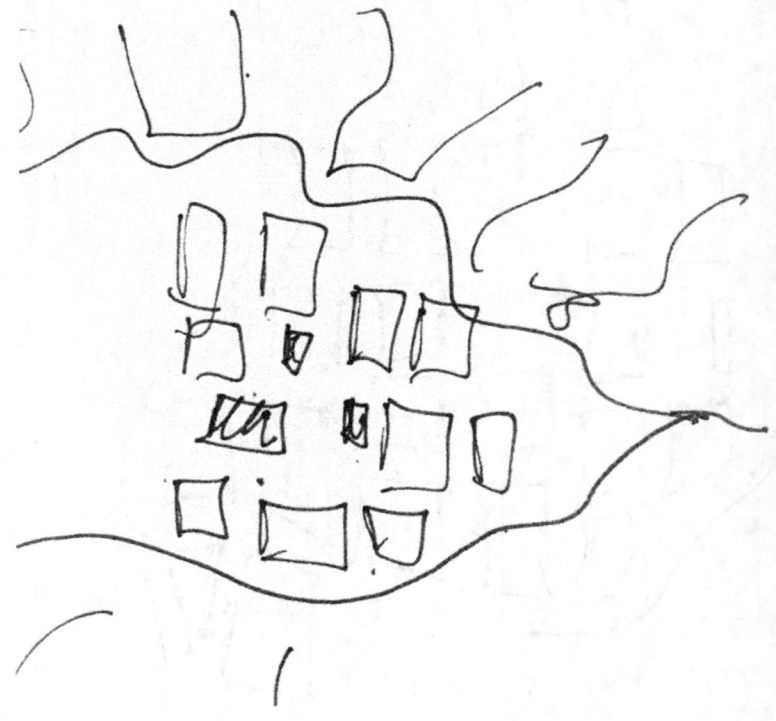

Pedro de Peralta founded the city in the high desert in 1608.

June 03
Bucaramanga 1622

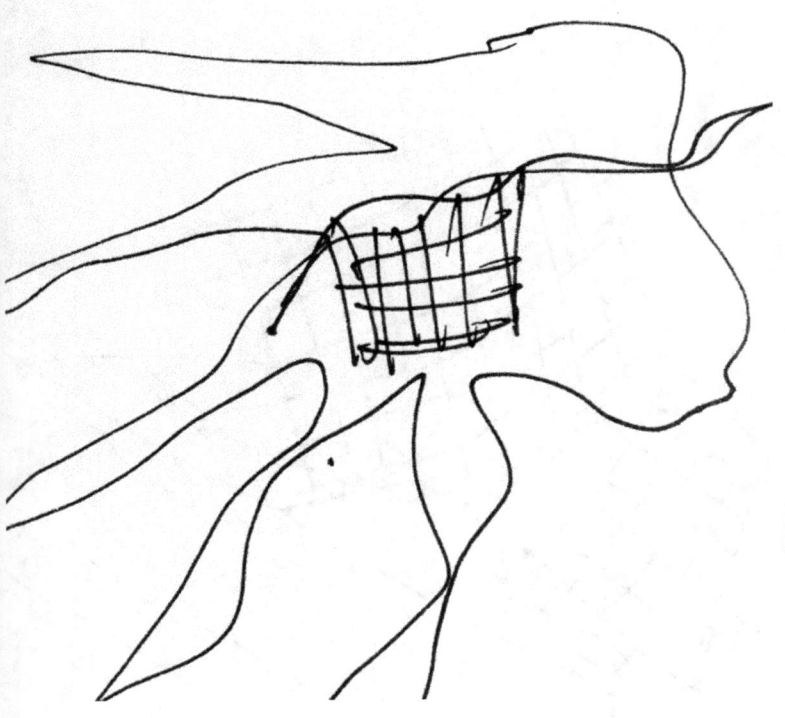

The Guane people inhabited the place nowadays known as Santander, before the city of Bucaramanga was founded.

June 04
Barranquilla 1629

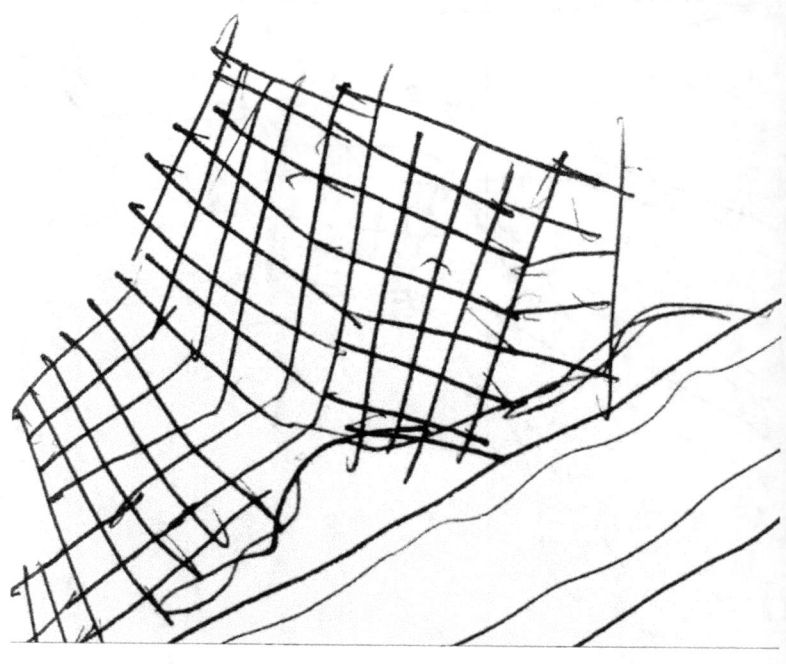

The Kamash lived in the cliffs (barrancas) where the Spanish founded Baranquilla de Camacho.

June 05
Paranaguá 1633

Paranaguá, or great round sea in Tupi, was settled by the Portuguese in the 1640s.

June 06
Luque 1635

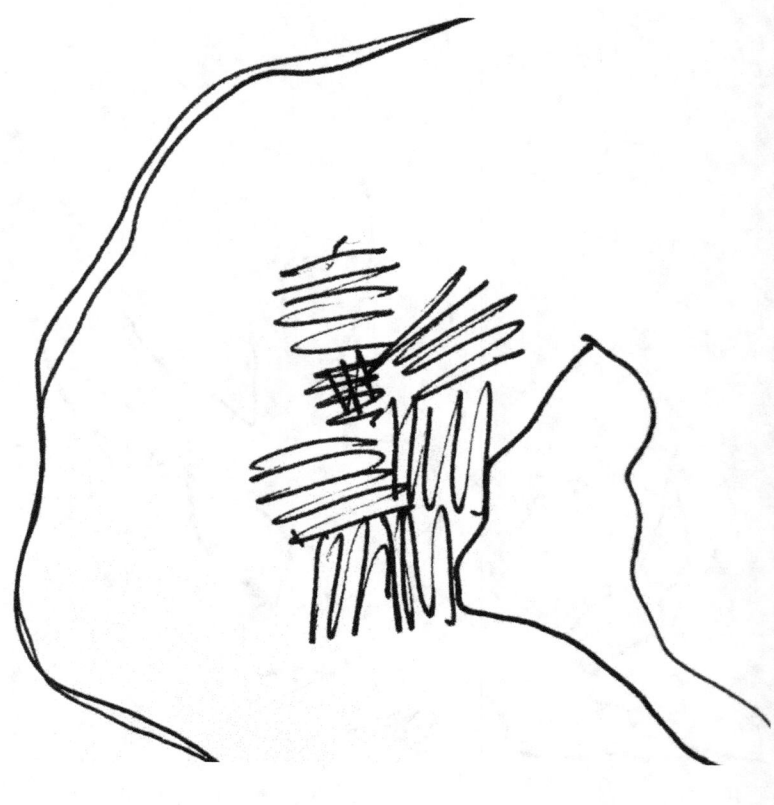

The lands by the Paraguay river were given to Miguel Antón de Luque in 1635.

June 07
Sorocaba 1661

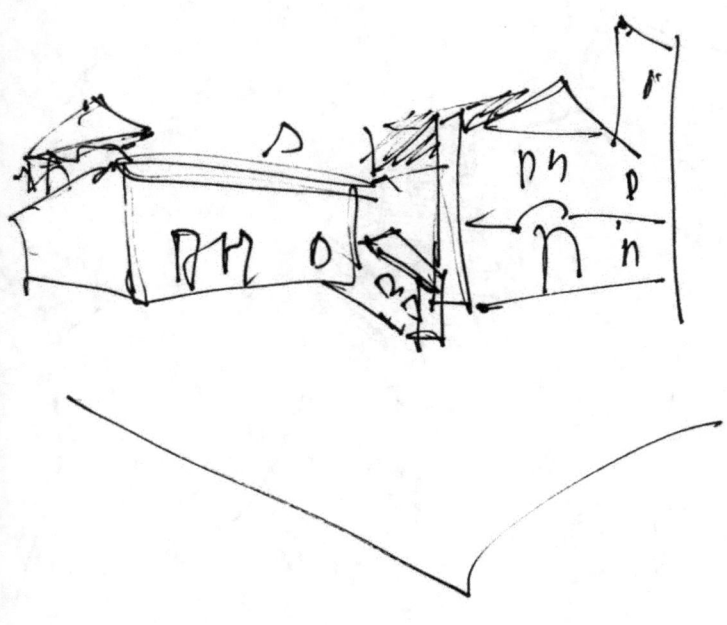

The Tupiniquins called that river Sorok (rippled) and the Portuguese named their city Sorocaba.

June 08
San Francisco 1766

The town of Yerba Buena was founded in 1766 by Spanish settlers, later renamed San Francisco.

June 09
Intanhaém

Plate of rock in Tupi is the meaning of Intanhaém.

June 10
Santarém

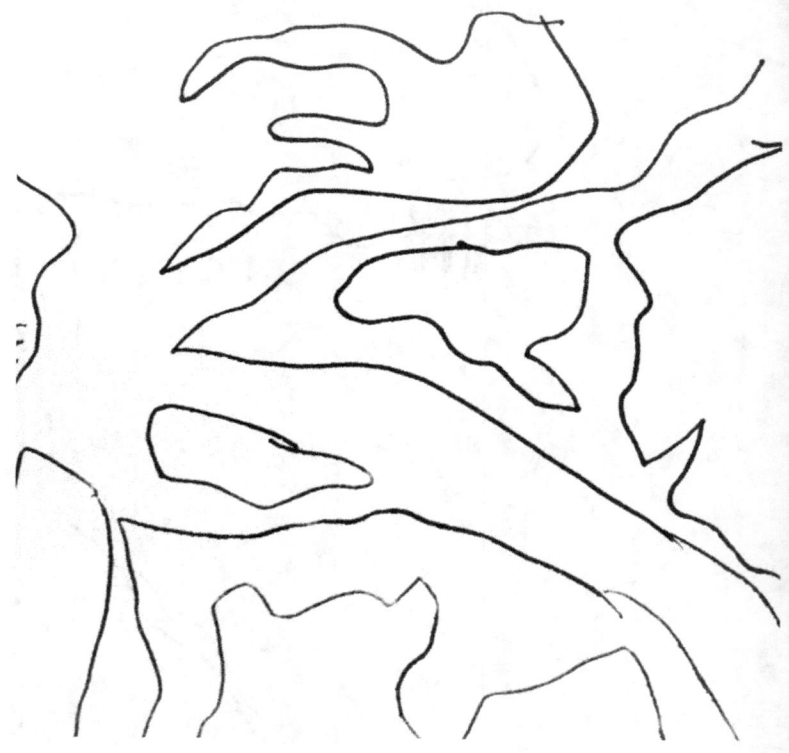

Five hundred miles upriver from the Amazon Delta the Portuguese created a fortification and named it Santarem after a city in their homeland.

June 11
Iguapé

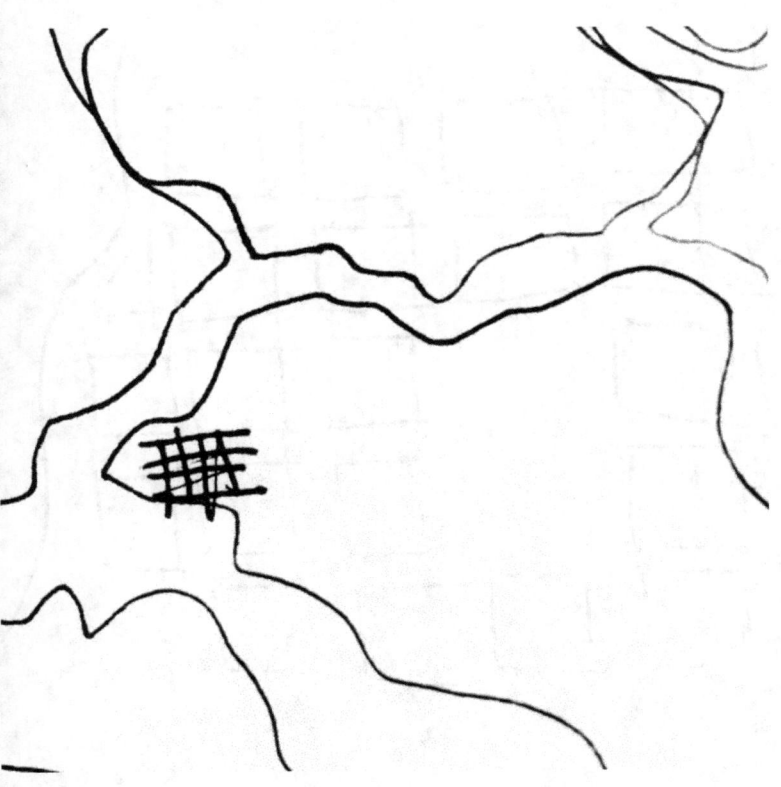

Y (water), Kua (delta) and Pe (at) in Tupi makes At the River Delta the meaning of Iguape, occupied by the Portuguese in the 1530s.

June 12
Quilmes

Southwest of Buenos Aires is the city of Quilmes, names after the Kilmes tribe of the northern plains.

June 13
La Candelária de Medellin 1675

Founded as "el poblado" in 1616, it was renamed Nuestra Senhora de la candelaria de Medellin in 1675.

June 14
El Paso

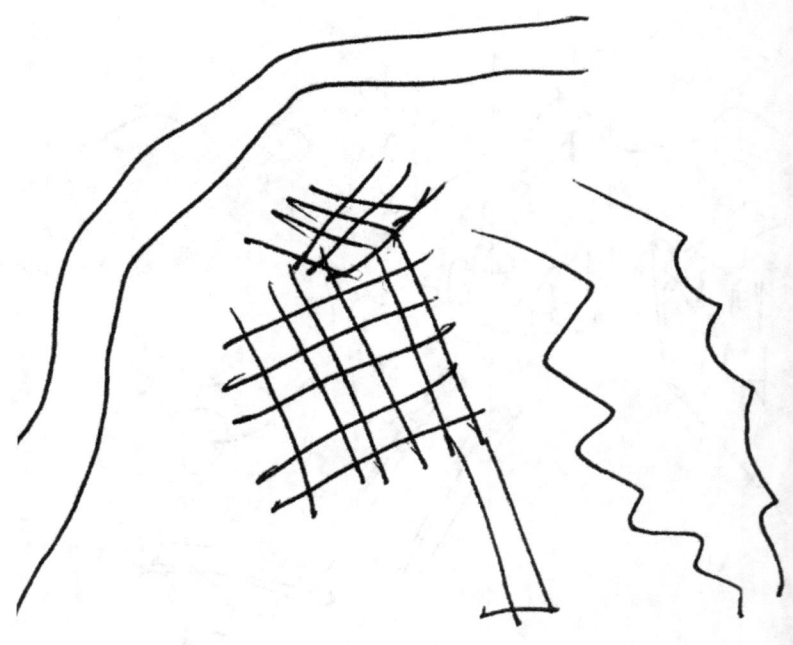

Mansos and Sumas lived on the banks of the Rio Bravo before the spanish named the river and the crossing sand banks El Paso del Norte.

June 15
Rosario

The Cachaqui people were already being forced to live in "reduciones" when the settlement of Pago de los Arroyos was renamed as Rosario.

June 16
Knoxville

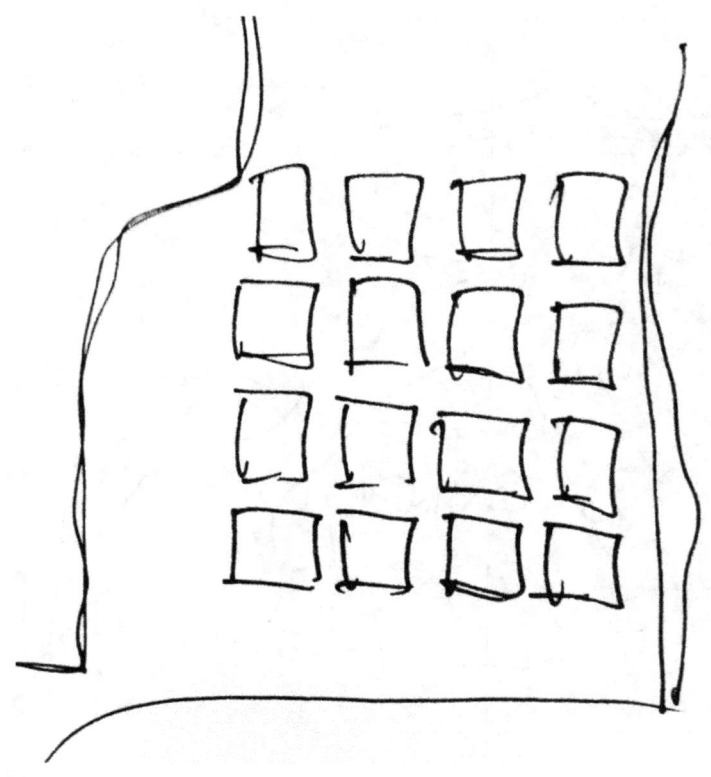

The Cherokee names their river Tennessee way before the Anglo settlers arrived, controled the river and built a city named after Washignton's War secretary Henry Knox.

June 17
Matanzas

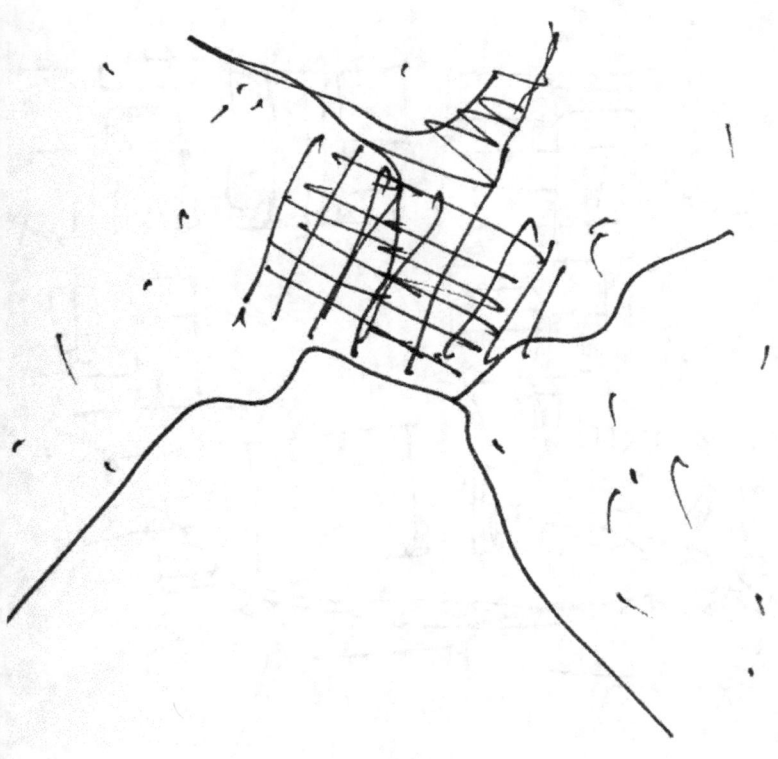

Matanzas, Cuba, is named after the occasion in 1510 in which 30 Spanish soldiers drowned after forcing local Taino fisherman to transport them accross the bay.

June 18
New Haven

The Quinnipiack lived in the area occupied by the puritans who justified their invasion of 1638 as a Christian Utopia.

June 19
Baltimore

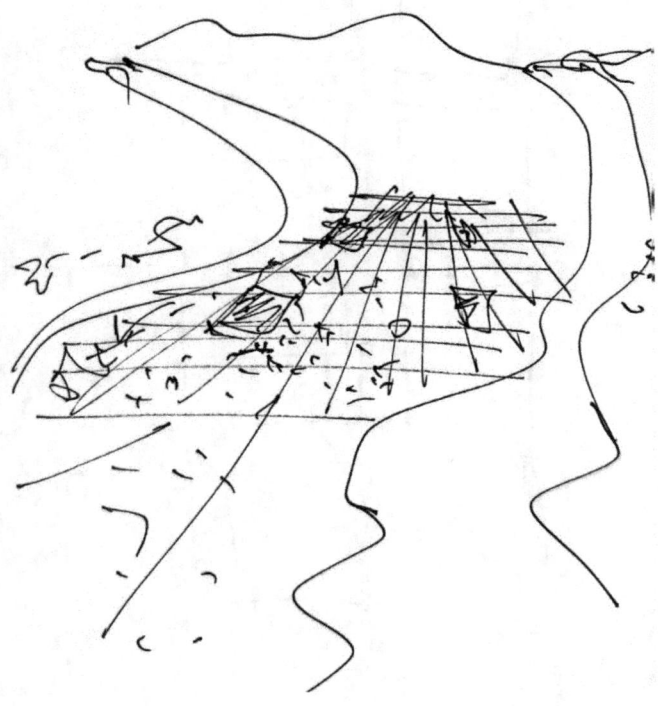

The Irish named this port city Baile an Tí Mhóir: big house town.

June 20
Tallahassee 1695

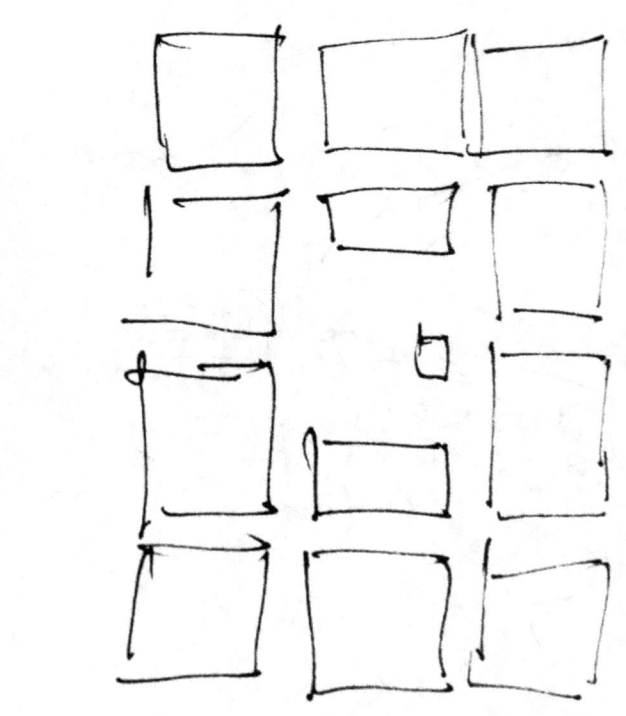

Tallahassee means "old fields" in Apalachee language, and that was precisely the area claimed by Hernando de Soto's expedition of 1539.

June 21
Talca

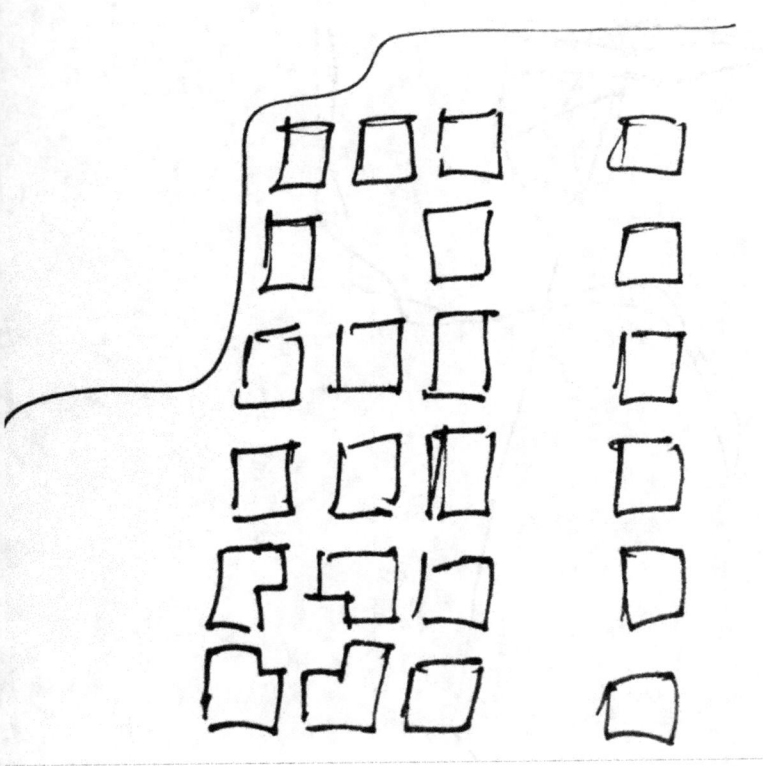

San Agustin de Talca was created in 1742 as part of a 250 year war of attrition between the Spanish and the Mapuche.

June 22
Ponce

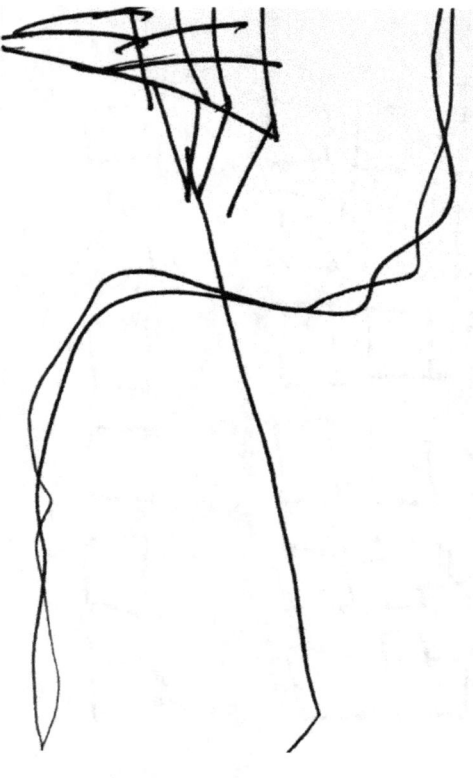

Named after Ponce de Leon to commemorate 200 years of the Spanish conquer in 1692.

June 23
Quebec

Kebec, in the Algonquin language means "where the river narrows."

June 24
Port Royal, Nova Scotia

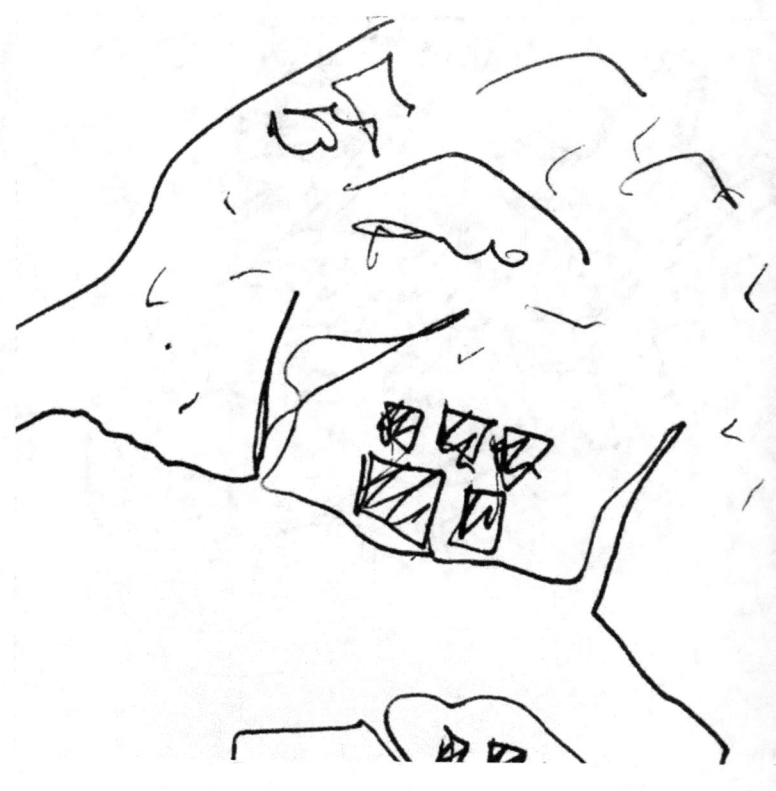

Originally named Acadia, Port Royal was the first French settlement in North America.

June 25
Plymouth

The first Puritan separatists arrived in 1620 making a treaty with the Wampanoag that would soon be broken.

June 26
Salvaterra

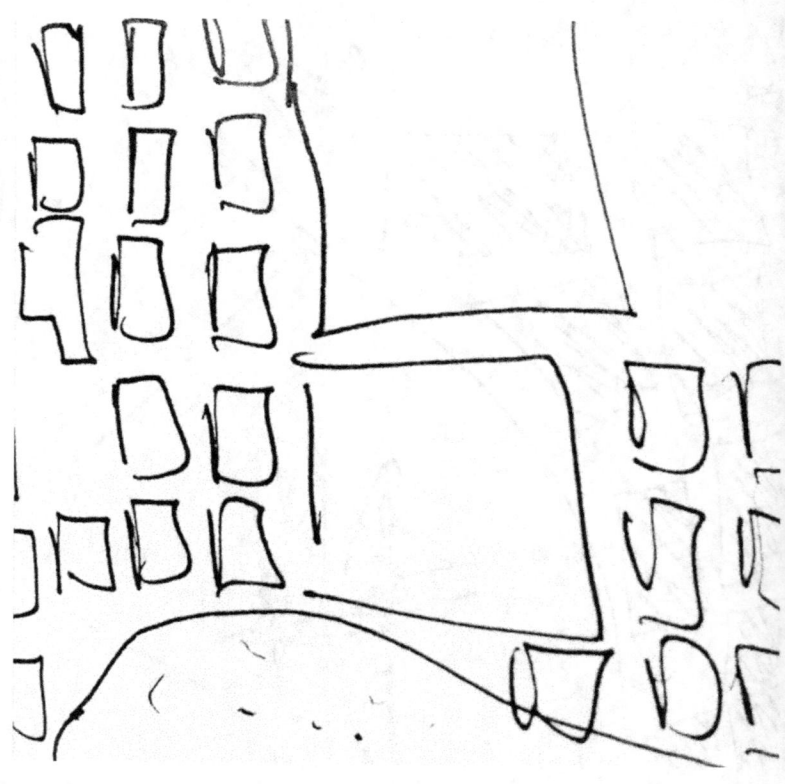

The Purépecha, and before them the Chichimeca inhabited the valley of Huatzindeo, where Franciscan friars renamed Salvaterra a century later.

June 27
Concepción

Known as La Frontera until the 1870s because south of the Bio Bio river the teritory was controlled by the Mapuche.

June 28
Sisoguichi

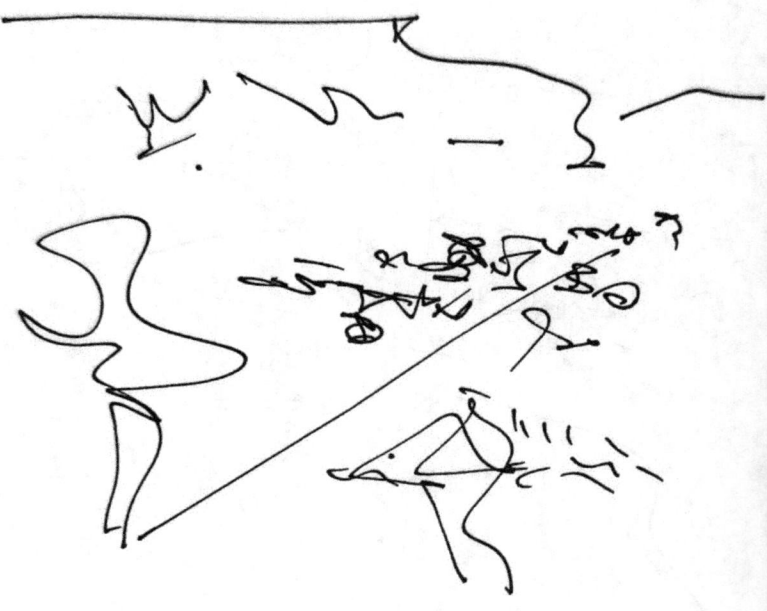

The hill of Taharumara, named after its original inhabitants, hosted the Jesuits who named the site Sisoquichic - place of arrows.

June 29
Juticalpa

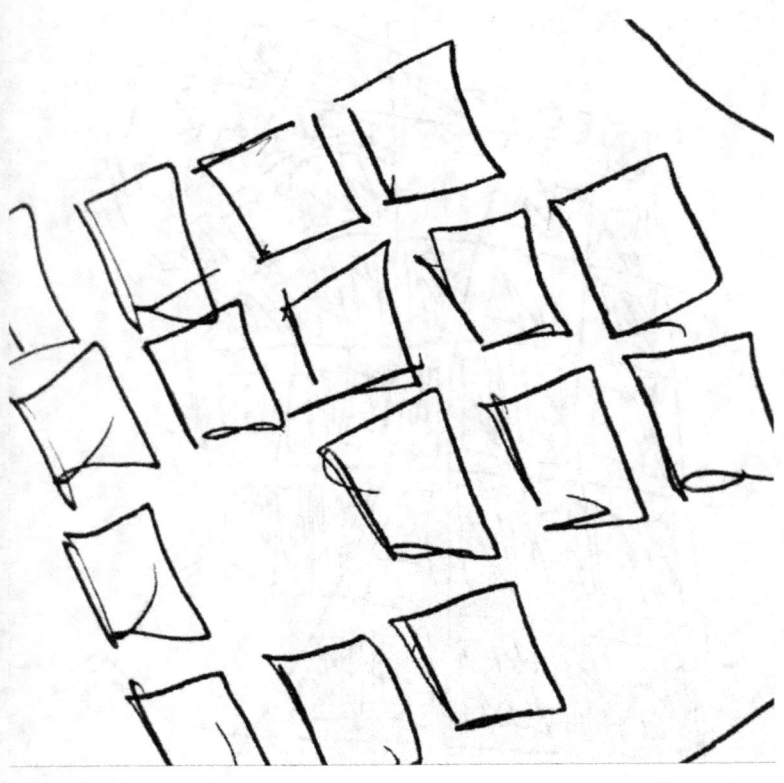

The silver mines of Guayape were served by the agricultural town of Juticalpa - in Nahuatl snail home.

June 30
Santa Rosa

The Poeceo people inhabited the lands by the Zaruma gold mines where the Spanish created Santa Rosa in the 16th century.

July 01
Vila Rica

The Itacolomi rock (stone boy in Tupi) helped the bandeirantes remember the creek where they found gold in 1695.

July 02
Glaura

Hungry miners blinded by the gold rush needed food that was cultivated in Glaura.

July 03
Mariana

Less than 10 miles separate the intellectual and libertine Ouro Preto from the pious Mariana.

July 04
Sertões de Taubaté

Hundreds of miles north of Taubaté the paulistas tried to claim the mines as their domain.

July 05
Congonhas

Congoi in Tupi means "the one who feeds", another city created to support hungry miners.

July 06
São José del Rey

A rocky hill separated São José from Sáo João, both cities dedicated to El Rey.

July 07
Sabará

Sabarabuçu means large shinny rock in Tupi, the name given to this hill full of metals.

July 08
São João Del Rey

Arraial Novo do Rio das Mortes - new village on death river was the name given to this place between 1701 and 1713.

July 09
Santa Bárbara

The creek rich with gold was named after Santa Barbara because the Portuguese arrived there on her day of December 4th, 1704.

July 10
Serro

Cold Hill - Serro do Frio was the name given to the place in 1702.

July 11
Roças Novas

Roças Novas means new cultivation, another city built to feed the miners.

July 12
São Brás

Suasu y means deer creek in Tupi, the name of the water added to an Armenian saint from the 4th century CE.

July 13
São Gonçalo do Rio das Pedras

Visions of a saint under a guava tree justify naming this town after this Portuguese priest from the 12th century cannonized in 1551

July 14
Morro Vermelho

Rich in iron ore, the earth of Minas Gerais has different tones of red from oxidation, thus the name Red Hill.

July 15
Vila Boa de Goiás

The Tupi called themselves gwaya - people that are my equal, my fellow.

July 16
Barão de Cocais

Morro Grande - big hill was the name of this town before the Brazilian government renamed it after a local landowner.

July 17
Bento Rodrigues
(destroyed by mud in 5 Nov 2015)

The small town of Bento Rodrigues, right downriver from a large Vale iron ore mine, was destroyed by a mudslide in Nov 5th, 2015.

July 18
Acurí

Acuru y means pebble creek in Tupi.

July 19
Dom Joaquim

Rio do Peixe - fish river - was the
original name of this place.

July 20
São Gotardo

Gotardo de Hildemshein, born in the 10th century, names this place in Minas Gerais, 700 years and 6500 of miles away.

July 21
Monsenhor Horta

Most mining cities were named after original Tupi words, catholic saints or local prists such as Horta, Joaquim or Isidro.

July 22
Amarantina

$(Fe^{3+})_2O(SO_4)_2(H_2O)_4 \cdot 3H_2O$
is the chemical compost
commonly called Amarantina
- usually indicates gold
formations nearby

July 23
Nossa Sra dos Córregos

Our Lady of the Creeks was probably invoked to protect miners who worked with their legs deep in the water.

July 24
Monsenhor Isidro

Another small mining village named after a local bishop.

July 25
Diamantina

Diamond Town, the names explains the reason the Portuguese exterminated the Malalis and Copoxós who lived there earlier.

July 26
Alto Maranhão

Arraial do Redondo - round village - was the 18th century name of this town.

July 27
São Felipe

Felipe Neri, italian clergy of the 16th century, named this mining village.

July 28
Camargos

Named after the marshy lands of Camargue, south of France, the Camargos family came to Mines Gerais in the 18th century.

July 29
Cachoeira do Campo

A waterfall on the Itabirito river named this town.

July 30
Sopa

The original name of the land of Iviturí, renamed Sopa by the diamond miners of the late 18th century.

July 31
Santa Rita Durão

Inficionado (infected) was the name of this village, renamed after a poet born there in 1722.

August 01
Zacatecas

The original inhabitants retained the name of this region where 200,000 tons of silver were extracted since the Spanish invasion.

August 02
Pachuca

Patiachiucan means "narrow place" in Nahuatl, another rich silver mining place in operation since the Aztecs ruled the region.

August 03
Guanajuato

Guamare or "children of the wind" were the name of the original inhabitants of Cuanaxhuato - the hill of frogs in Nahuatl.

August 04
San Luis Potosi

San Luis de Mezquitique was the name of this mining town before being renamed for its southern (Bolivian) counterpart.

August 05
Carabaya

The Aymara called this mountain range Kallawaya, meaning place of the healers.

August 06
Copiapó

The Diaguita people were the last of 10,000 years of occupation of those lush lands that the Spanish explored for silver in the 18th century.

August 07
Chachapoias

The Chachapoyas lived at the headwaters of the Marañon-Amazon river, at the eastern flanks of the Andes

August 08
Antofagasta

Town of the great salt lake in the
indigenous Cacan language.

August 09
Popayan

Po Pa Yan means village of reed roofs, the name of the original settlement of the Sonso culture.

August 10
Tegucigalpa

Taguz Galpa means silver hill in Nahuatl, another city founded by resource exploitation.

August 11
Tehuantepec

Jaguar Mountain was the original name of this Zapotec town that named the Isthmus.

August 12
Sultepec

The land is called Tolomostas but the Spanish renamed it San Antonio de las Invernadas.

August 13
Hualgayoc

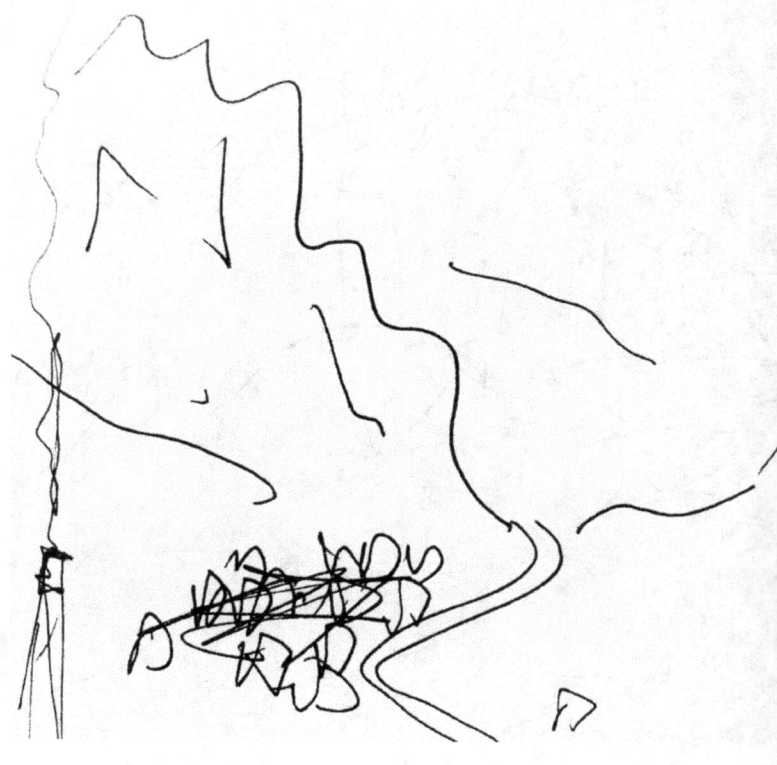

City in the Plains is the Ayamara meaning of Hualgayoc.

August 14
Tlapujahua

Inhabited by the Mazahuas,
Tlalpujahua means spongy

August 15
Zaruma

Meaning corn (sara) head (uma) in Quechua, Zaruma was built by the Cañari people around the year 500 CE.

August 16
Zumpango

Tzompanco, Nahuatl for Row of Hair is the name of this settlement at the margins of a lake of the same name, occupied by different ethnic groups for over 3000 years.

August 17
Oruro

The Uro Uro people lived in the area rich in silver, renamed Oruro by the Spanish conquerors.

August 18
Cerro de Pasco

At 14,000 ft above sea level, Cerro de Pasco became known as "men-eating-mountain" after the Spanish forced the indigenous to work the mines.

August 19
Valdivia

The southernmost city of Spanish America, Valdivia is home to the Monte Verde fossils that challenge the Clovis theory of human occupation in the Americas.

August 20
Huencavelica

Spanish miners tried to call the site Vila Rica de Oropesa but native workers insisted in calling is Huancavelica, from Quechua Wankawillka.

August 21
San Antonio del Nuevo Mundo

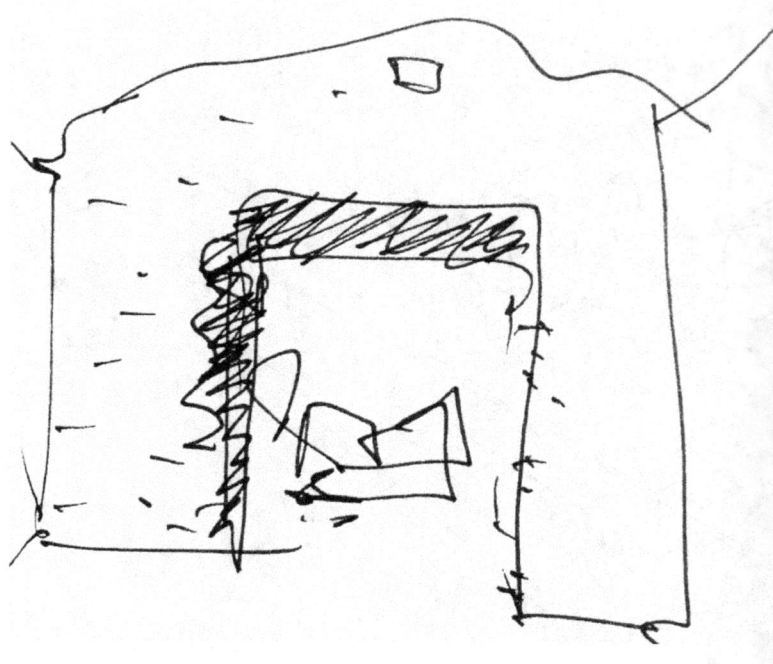

In Uyuni, Bolivia, sits the now abandoned mining town of San Antonio del Nuevo Mundo.

August 22
Castrovirreyna

Named Chuqlluqucha or Coyca Palca in Quechua, the town of Castrovirreyna gave the Spanish enough silver to pave an entire street

August 23
Nóvita

The first Spanish capital of the Choco province, Nóvita was created around a gold mine worked by enslaved Africans

August 24
Parral

Silver mines were found in the land of the Conchos, today's Parral, Chihuahua.

August 25
Colima

Coliman means "place of the ancestors" in Nahuatl, a city by the Pacific ocean in the vicinity of a volcano of the same name: Coliman - the grandfather.

August 26
Valdivia

On May 22, 1960, the most powerful earthquake in recorded history with a magnitude of 9.5 struck Valdivia, killing 5,000 people.

August 27
Lota

The mining town of Lota has a
beautiful female-led movement
for the preservation of its
industrial heritage.

August 28
Batopilas

The Raramuri people called that site Bachotigori, place of the enclosed waters.

August 29
Zimapan

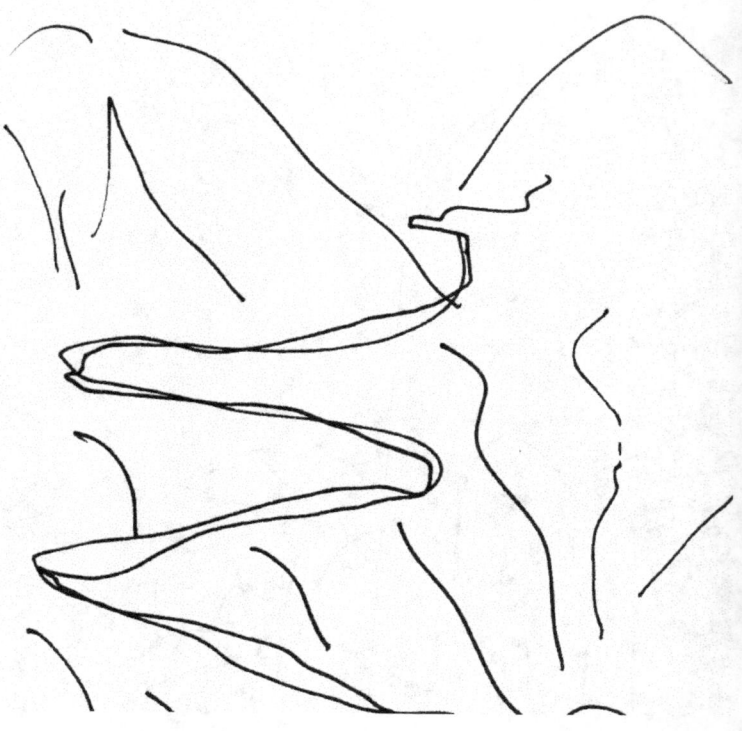

Cimatl + Pan means the place of the pulque roots, in Nathatl.

August 30
Texco

Tlachco means the place of the ball game, another mining town in Central Mexico.

August 31
Real del Monte

The Real del Monte strike of 1766 is considered be the first real labor strike in North American history.

September 01
Boston Harbor 1773

American colonists dumped 342 chests of tea in the water to protest taxation.

September 02
Concord 1775

The first shots of the American revolutionary war happened in Concord, Massachusetts, April 19, 1775.

September 03
Saratoga 1777

The battle of Saratoga, NY, in October of 1777 gave the American revolutionary a much needed morale boost.

September 04
Tupac Amaru 1780

José Gabriel Condorcanqui – known as Túpac Amaru II, led a revolt against the Spanish in Peru, 1780.

September 05
Oruro 1781

Two parallel rebelions, one by locals of Spanish descent (creolos) and another by Andean people shoked the mining town of Oruro in 1781.

September 06
Haiti 1791

What would be the first succesfull rebellion of Black People in the Americas started in Haiti in 1791.

September 07
Alfaiates 1798

The revolt of the tailors (Alfaiates in Portuguese) in Salvador da Bahia, August 1798, attempted to free Brazil from Portugal.

September 08
San Lorenzo 1813

The first battle of the Argentinian independence war was fought in San Lorenzo, February of 1813.

September 09
Buenos Aires 1806

British forces managed to invade Buenos Aires in 1806 but were forced to retreat after street fights killed half their contingent.

September 10
Chuquisaca 1809

In May of 1809 the people of Chuquisaca (today Sucre, Bolivia) rebelled for self government.

September 11
Dolores 1810

On September 16, 1810, priest Miguel Hidalgo rang his church bell and called his people to rise against Spain.

September 12
Asencio 1811

In February of 1811 the people at the eastern banks of the Uruguay river (nowadays Uruguay) rallied in support of Buenos Aires' independence and against Spain.

September 13
Cucuta 1813

Simon Bolivar's vitory in Cucuta, February of 1813, gave the Gran Colombia independence movement the momentum it needed.

September 14
Chacabuco

After leading the independence war in Argentina, José de San Martín crossed the Andes to support the Chilean independence, beating the Spanish in Chacabuco, 1817.

September 15
Maipu

San Martin and O'Higgins joined forces against the Spanish and defeated them in Maipu, April 5, 1817.

September 16
Tacna 1811

Tacna was the first city in Peru to rebel against the Spanish in June of 1811.

September 17
Cartagena 1812

The Cartagena Manifesto, by Simon Bolivar, was written in that city on December 15, 1812.

September 18
Apatzingan

In the city dedicated to Apahtzï
- God of Death - the Mexican
revolutionary constitution was
signed on October 22, 1814.

September 19
Boyacá 1819

The independece of Nueva Granada / Gran Colombia, was sealed when the revolutionary army led by Bolivar won the battle of Boyaca in 1819.

September 20
Callao

The conquest of Callao in 1826
marked the end of Spanish rule
in South America.

September 21
Pichincha

The battle of Pichincha, at the foot of the volcano of the same name, established the independence of the province of Quito.

September 22
Maracaibo

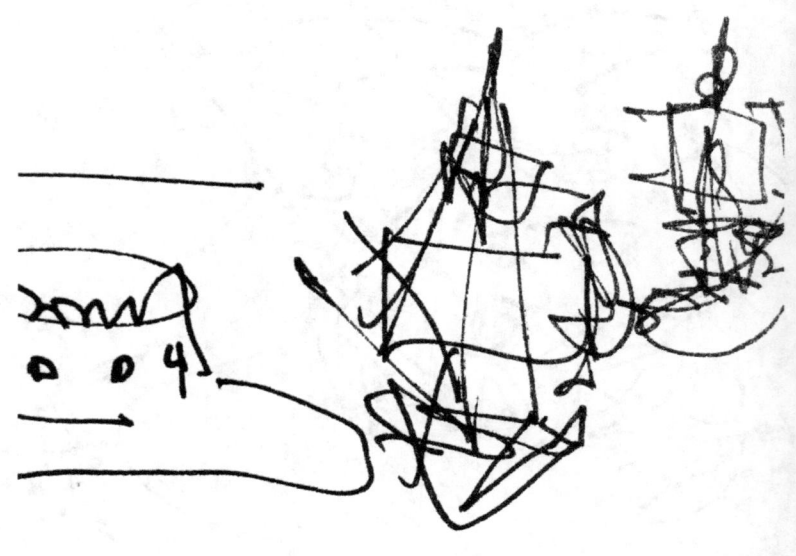

Spanish and revolutionary forces fought at Lake Maracaibo on July 24, 1823, with another major victory for Bolivar's movement.

September 23
Guayaquil

On October 9, 1820, the port city of Guayaquil - Wayakil in Quechua joined the independance movement.

September 24
Ayacucho

Callao was the last stronghold of Spanish Royalists in Peru, but the war was decided 2 years before, in Ayacucho.

September 25
Soriano

Cuba was fighting for independence since the Ten Years War of 1868-78, with Palma de Soriano in the south as one of the revolutionary centers.

September 26
Campo Maracanã

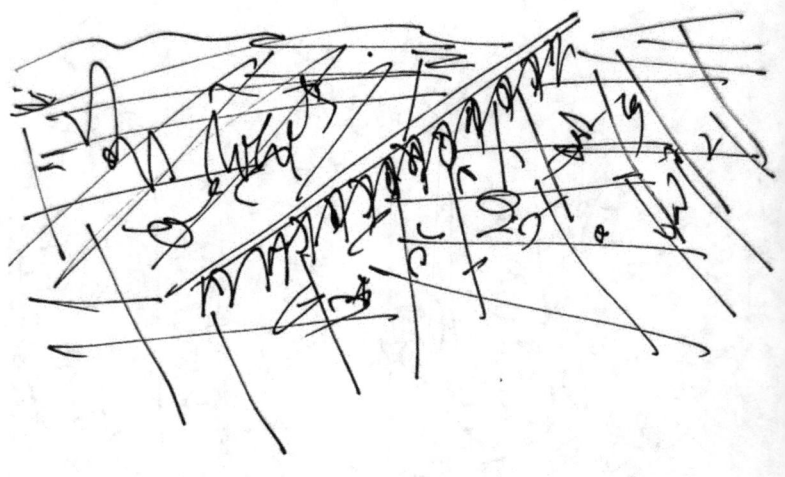

Maracanã is a bird that would become famous for other battles, this one won by the Argentinians in 1811.

September 27
Tampico

Mexicans and Yankees fought
together in 1835 against
Antonio Santa Anna.

September 28
Curupaity

In September of 1866 the Paraguayans held their positions in Curupaity, against superior forces of Argentina, Brazil and Uruguay.

September 29
Everywhere in Brazil 2018

September 30
Campichuelo

On 19 December 1810 the forces led by Manuel Belgrano conquered the Spanish garrison at Campichuelo on the Parana river.

October 01
Washington DC

The Piscataway lived there before the Maryland colonists and the 1783 rebellion in Philadelphia that pushed the revolutionary government in search of a new capital.

October 02
Louisiana Purchase

Following the Haitian revolution, Napoleon decided to sell his North American colonies, giving the young USA control of the conection between the Gulf of Mexico and the Great Lakes.

October 03
Jeffersonian grid

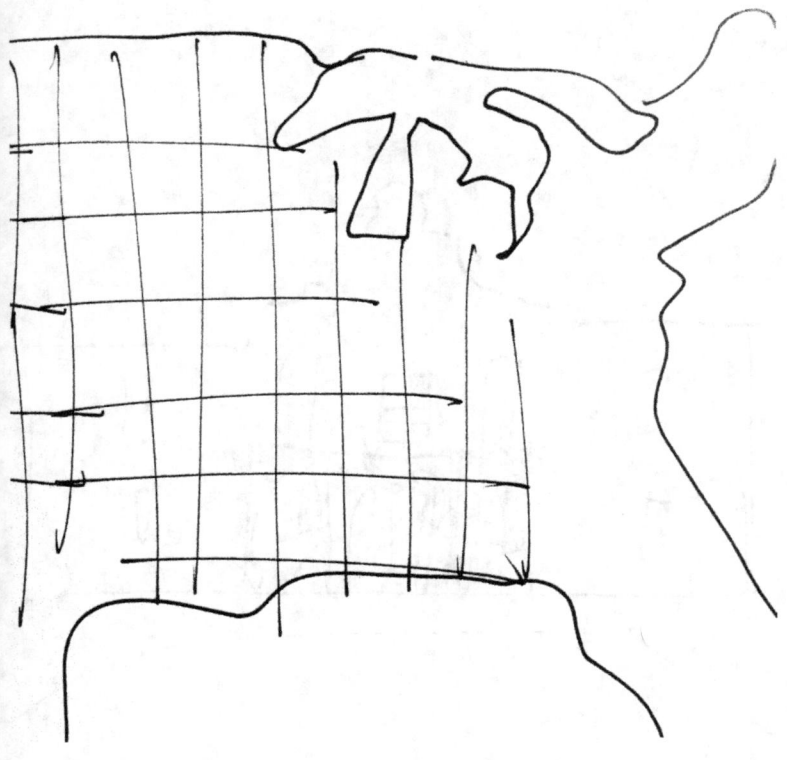

Land had to be abstracted into numbers and detached from those who lived there in order fit better into the capitalism system.

October 04
Fighting for slavery 1835

Anglo settlers in Tejas fought against Mexico in 1835 to be able to keep slavery in place.

October 05
Fighting for slavery again 1861

Anglo settlers in Texas, now joined with USA, fought again to keep slavery in place in 1861.

October 06
Saint Louis

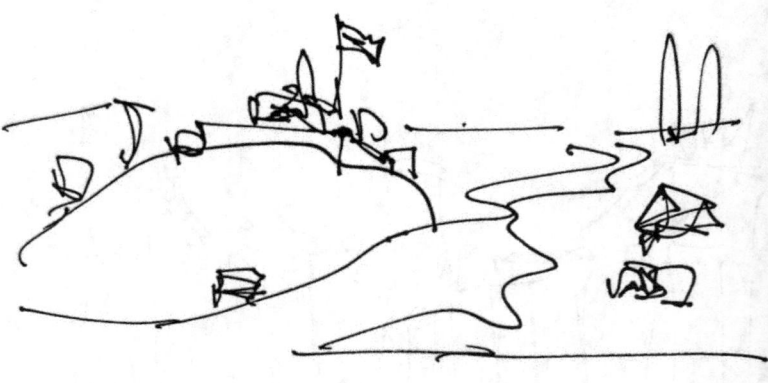

The encounter of 2 mighty rivers have attracted people for thousands of years.

October 07
Chicago

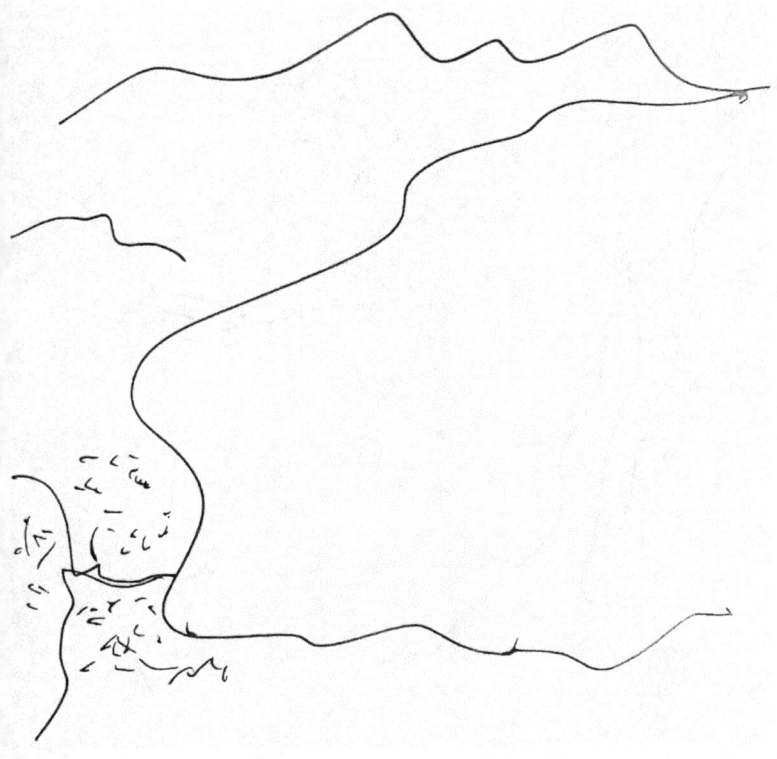

The marshland called shikaakwa connected the Great Lakes to the Gulf of Mexico.

October 08
Land Grabbing 1835

They already owned much
of the Tejas land in 1835 but
fought to keep slavery in place
and their lands profitable.

October 09
Land Grabbing 1848

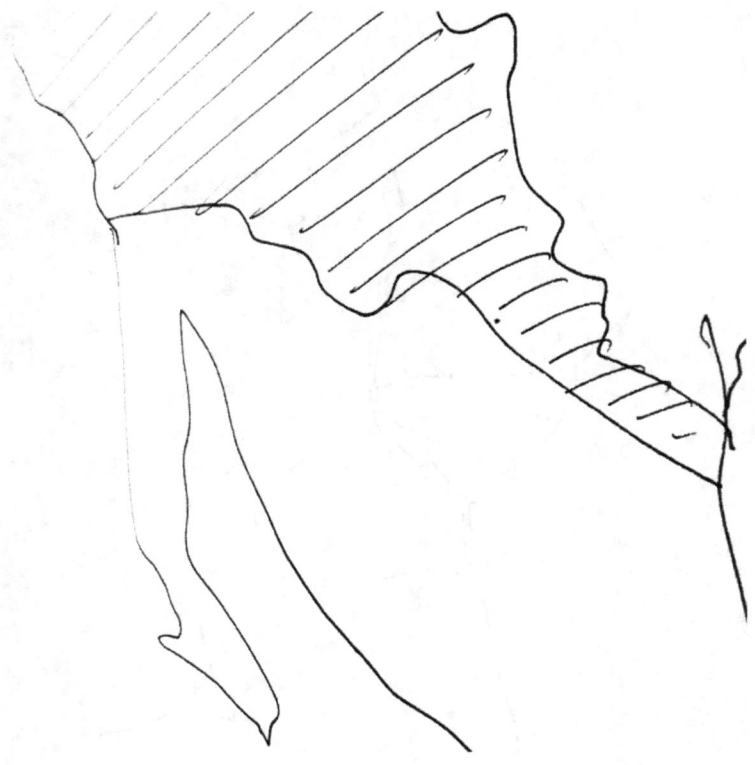

Half of the Mexican territory was taken by the USA army in 1848.

October 10
Land Grabbing 1865

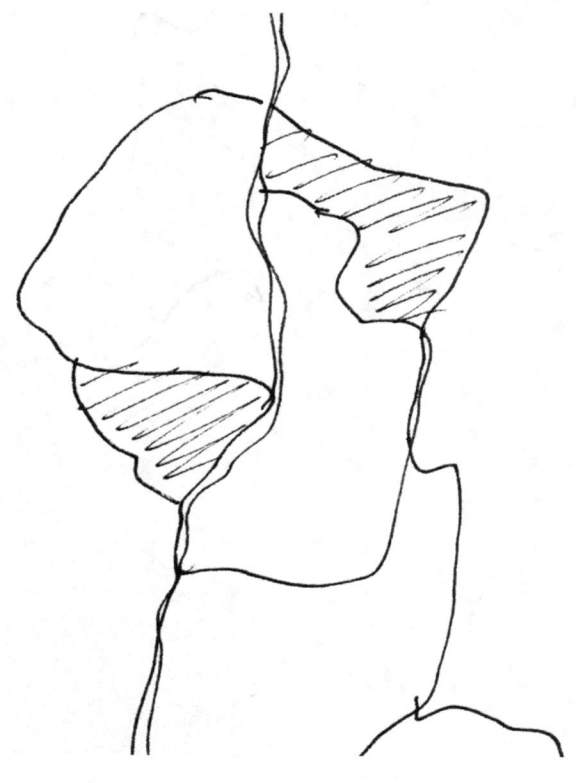

Brazil and Argentina grabbed half of Paraguayan territory in 1865.

October 11
Land Grabbing 1876

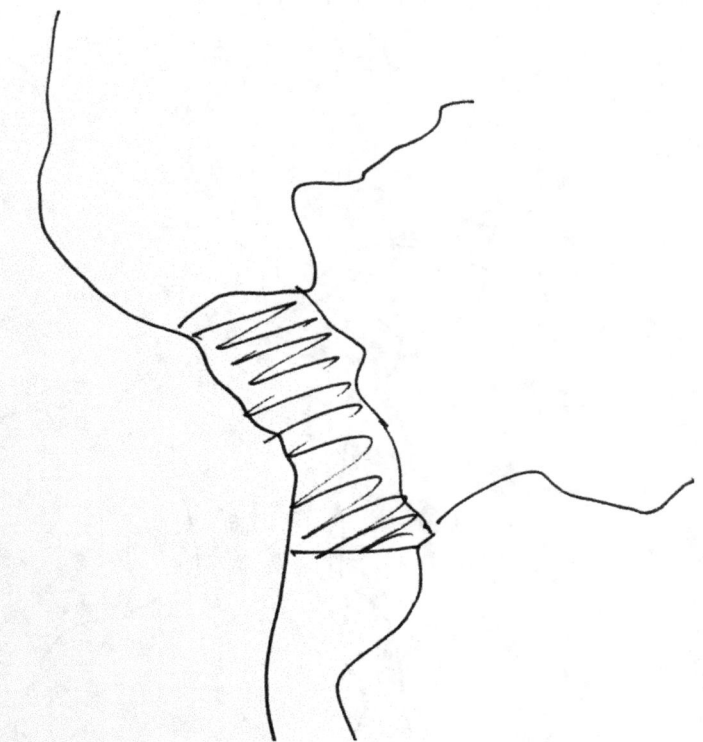

Chile invaded Bolivia and Peru in 1879, gaining access to saltpeter mines to make more gunpowder to make more wars.

October 12
Land Grabbing 1903

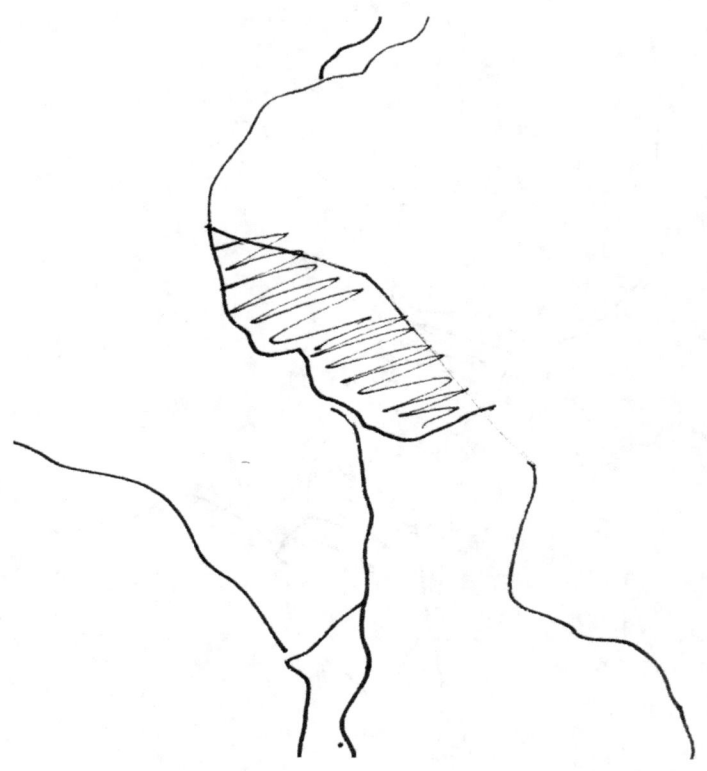

The young Brazilian republic took over the lands north of Acre River, previously controlled by Bolivia.

October 13
Amerindian Holocaust

On this day we remember that 90% of the Amerindian population died in the 16th century.

October 14

Orthogonal grid is a tool for land grabbing

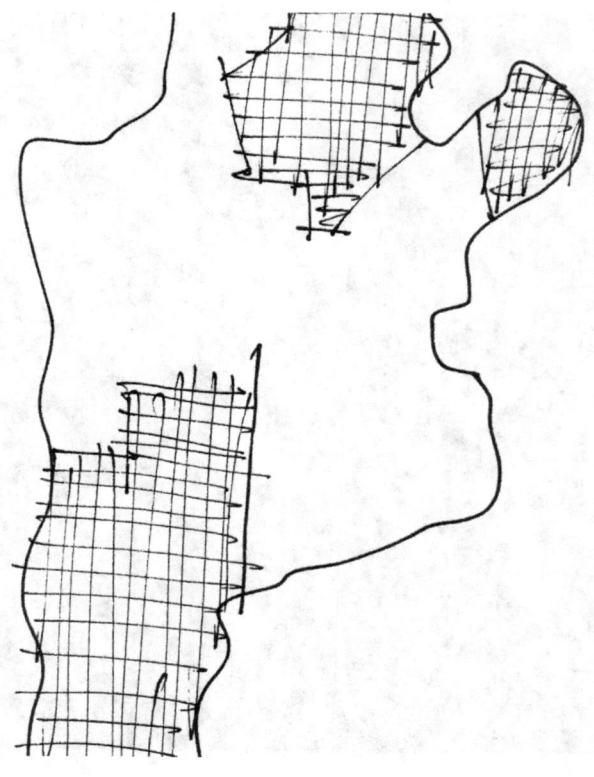

No caption needed here:
Orthogonal grid is a tool for
land grabbing.

October 15
New Orleans

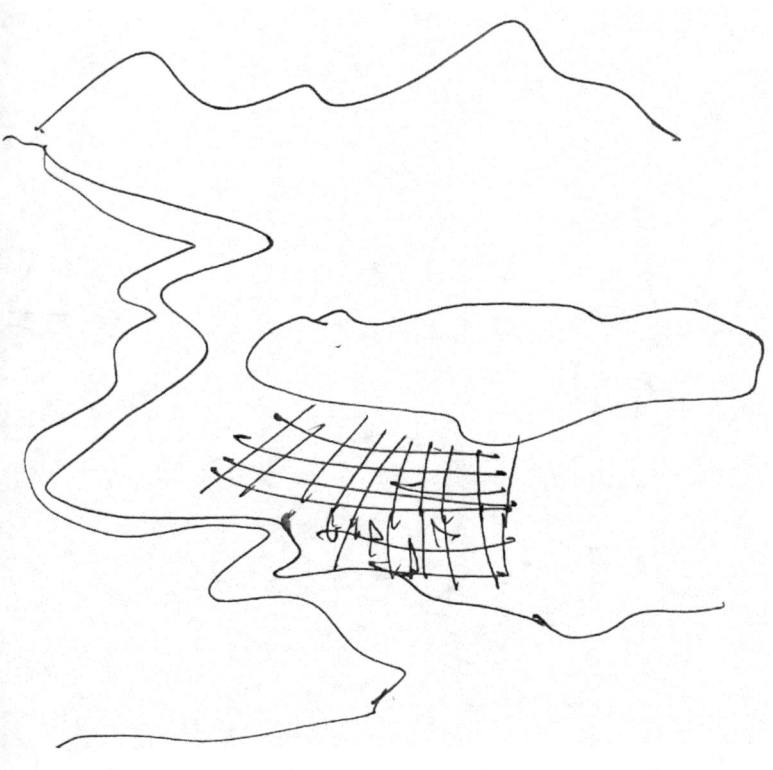

Sold due to the Haitian revolution, purchased by Tomas Jefferson, it has always been about white supremacy.

October 16
Rio de Janeiro 1808

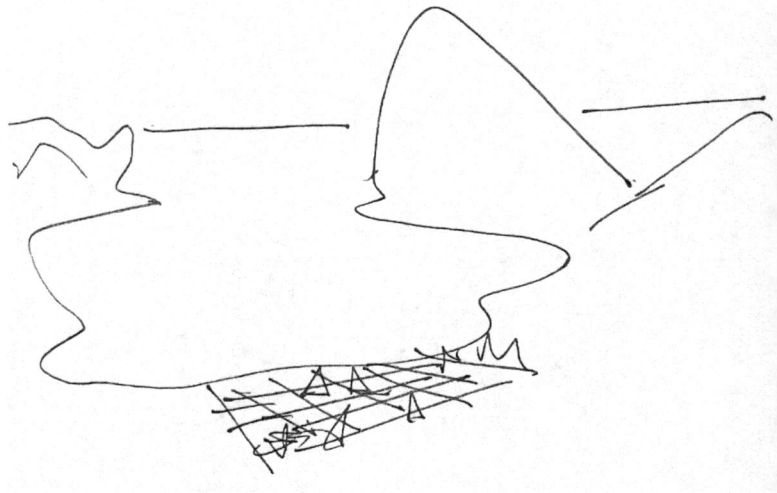

Fleeing Napoleon, the whole Portuguese court moved to Rio, making it the capital of an European Empire.

October 17
Guano

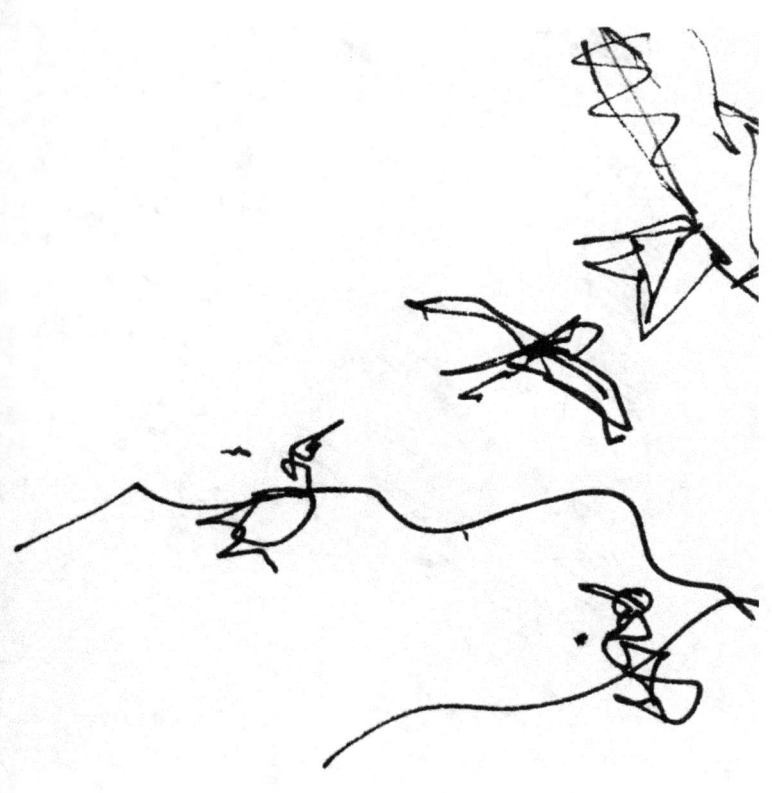

Chile, Bolivia and Peru fought for islands where they explored Guano in tehe 1860s.

October 18
Esclavitud abolida en Mexico 1829

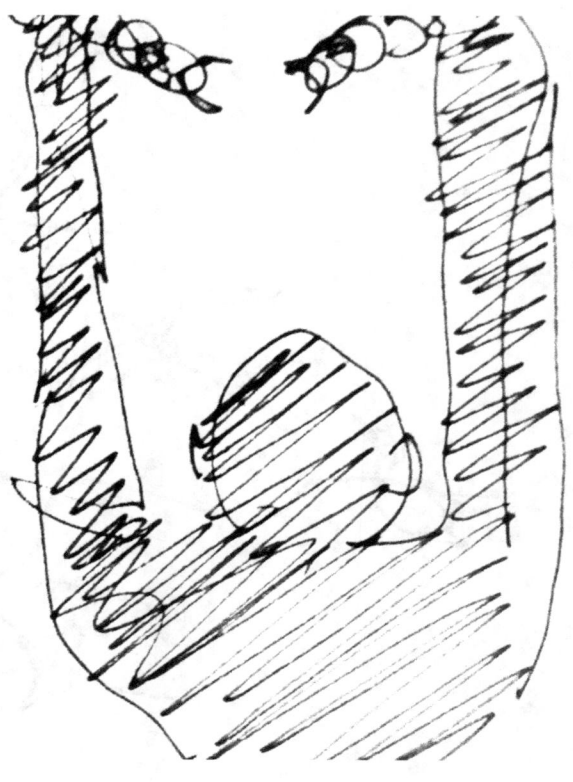

No caption needed here unless you have trouble understanding this as the cause of Texas independent movement a few years after.

October 19
Buenos Aires 1813

Argentina extends the vote to mestizos and indios, outlaws torture, slavery and the Inquisition.

October 20
Jenipapo 1823

Portugal tried to keep the Amazon separate from independent Brazil but lost a battle at Jenipapo, Piaui, 13 March 1823.

October 21
Homestead Act

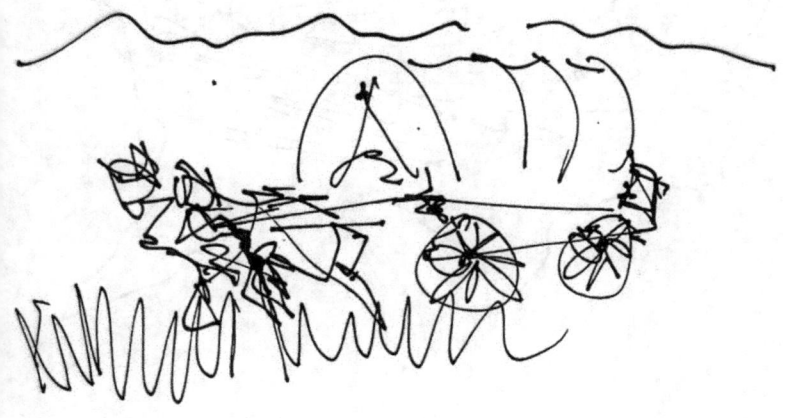

160 million acres (10 % of contemporary USA) was given free to 1.6 million white settlers as a result of the Homestead Act.

October 22
Nuestra Senhora de la Porciuncula

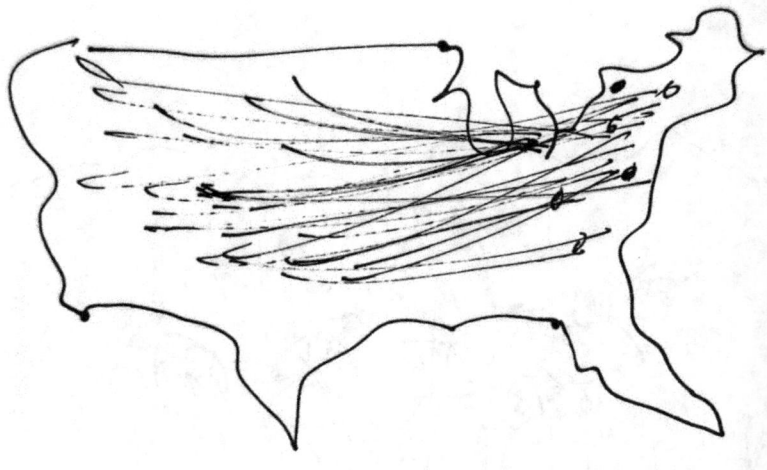

Anglo settlers start moving into Mexican California.

October 23
Lei de Terras 1850

Brazilian empire legalized private land ownership in 1850, but never surveyed the land to determine who owned what.

October 24
Oaxaca 1847

Benito Juarez, a Zapotec, is elected governor of Oaxaca.

October 25
Jose Marti 1895

José Marti was killed fighting the Spanish at the Battle of Dos Rios, Cuba, 19 May 1895.

October 26
Rio de Janeiro 1888

Regent princess Isabel signs
the law outlawing slavery
- the last country in the
Americas to do so.

October 27
Canudos 1897

The Brazilian government massacred a colony of destitute people who followed prophet Antonio Conselheiro in the backlands of Bahia.

October 28
Chaputepelc

France invaded Mexico and tried to re-colonize it, abandoning the idea after fierce resistance led by Benito Juarez.

October 29
Chicago 1870s

The city of Chicago was growing exponentially fast when a fire burned 25% of its structures in October of 1871.

October 30
Quinta da Boa Vista

Elias Antonio Lopez, slave trader, built the palace that would become the official residence of Brazilian emperors.

October 31
Chicago 1890s

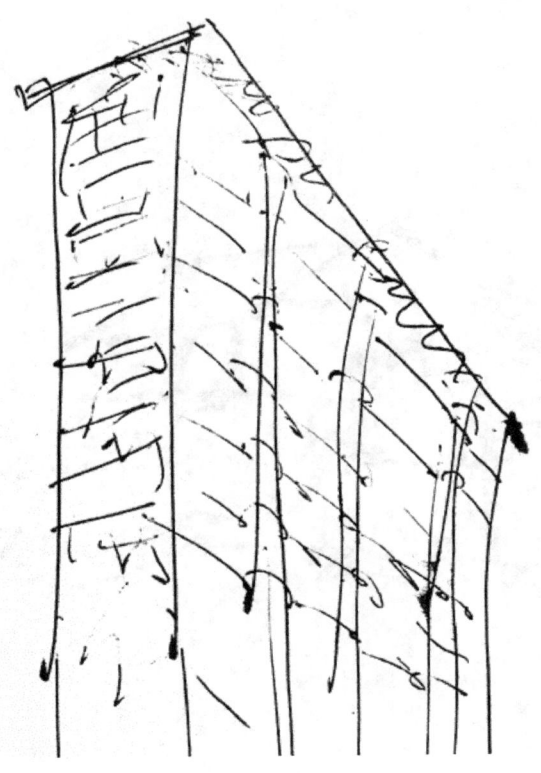

Bold architects and empowered speculators created the elevator and new structures to build skyscrappers.

November 01
San Juan 1915

Antoni Nechodoma brought
Frank Lloyd Wright's praire style
to Puerto Rico in 1915.

November 02
Estridentópolis 1925

German Cueto designed a city of the future (1975) based on the ideas of Estridentismo, a literary group led by Manuel Maples Arce.

November 03
San Angel 1931

Muralist Diego Rivera
comissioned architect Juan
O'Gorman a house/studio
complex for himself and his wife
Frida Kahlo.

November 04
Buenos Aires 1936

Corina Kavanaugh comissions a residential skyscrapper - tallest buildling in Latin America - for herself and her elite friends.

November 05
Montevideo 1936

Julio Vilamajó designs the Engineering School building for Universidad de la Republica, Montevideo.

November 06
Mar del Plata 1942

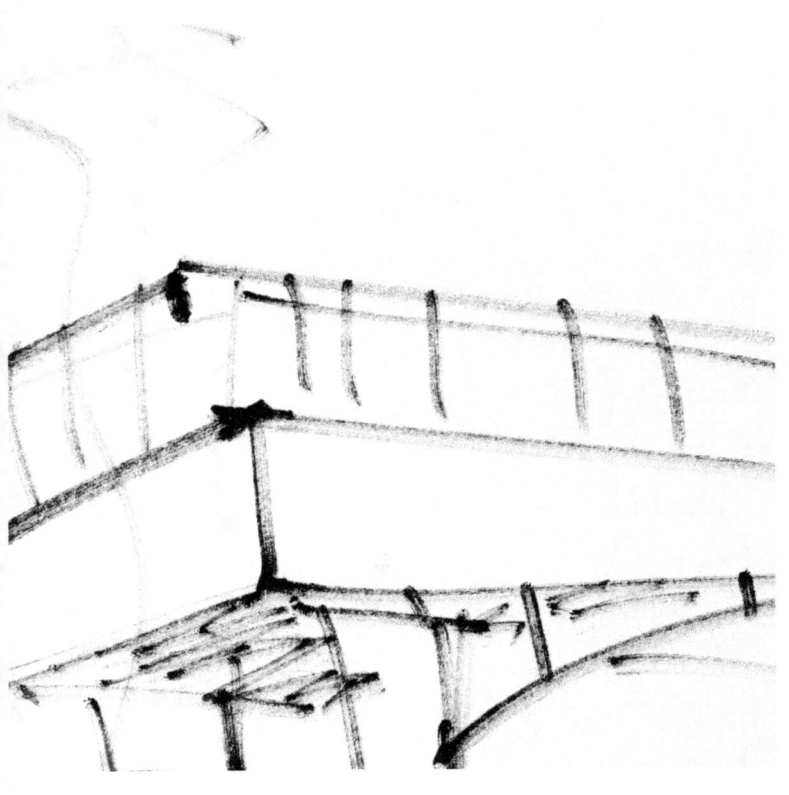

While an architect in the north designed a house over a waterfall, Amancio Williams designed one over a creek, with a much more modern plan.

November 07
Rio de Janeiro 1946

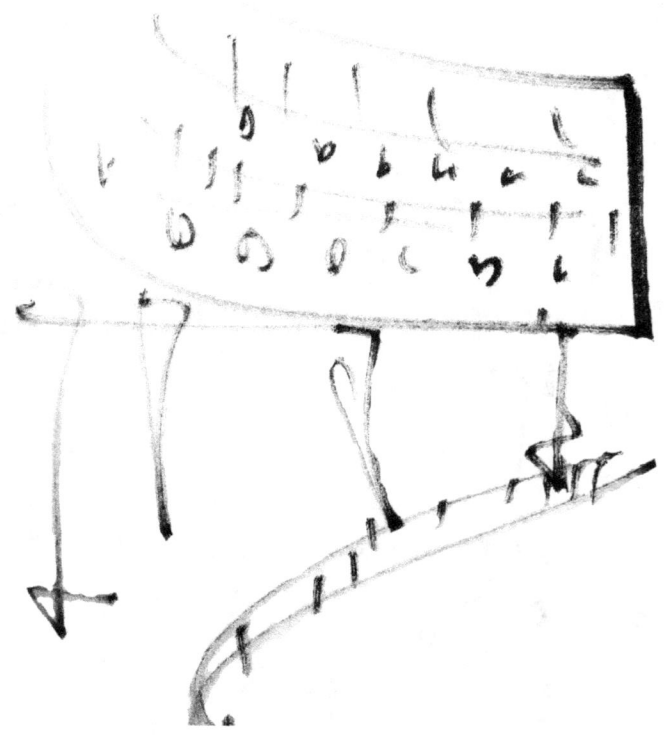

Affonso Reidy and Carmen Portinho built Pedregulho, an avantgarde housing complex in Rio de Janeiro.

November 08
New York 1947

A workshop of ten architects united in NYC to design the headquarters of the United Nations choose Oscar Niemeyer's scheme among all others.

November 09
Ciudad de México 1947

In Ciudad de Mexico, architect Mario Pani designed the Multifamiliar Miguel Aleman.

November 10
Pampulha 1943

Oscar Niemeyer changed the history of modern archietcture with a few lines.

November 11
Atlântida 1952

Eladio Dieste decided to be an architect in order to be a good catholic, and thus built the most amazing church.

November 12
Ciudad de Mexico 1953

Felix Candella explored thin vaults to build all kinds of programs in Mexico.

November 13
Caracas 1955

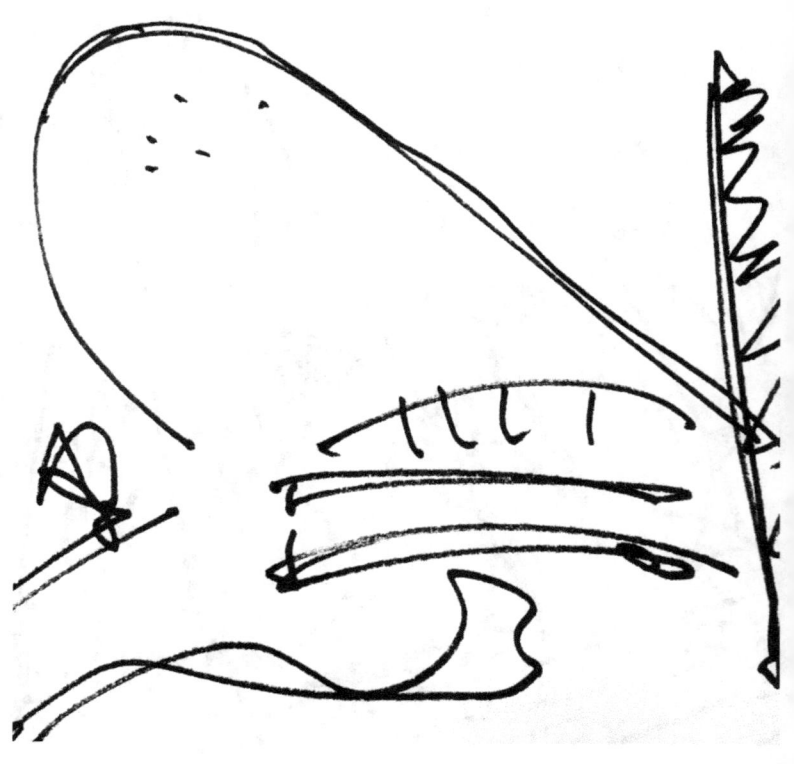

Fruto Vivas explores the parabolic vault to maximize the grand view of Caracas.

November 14
São Paulo 1957

Lina Bo Bardi elevates part of a museum, buries another part and creates a civic plaza for São Paulo.

November 15
Montevideo 1962

Carlos Bayardo designs the most elegant builllding for the dead.

November 16
Ciudad de México 1964

Pedro Ramirez Vasquez builds
a monument to Mexican
indigenous cultures.

November 17
Guatemala 1971

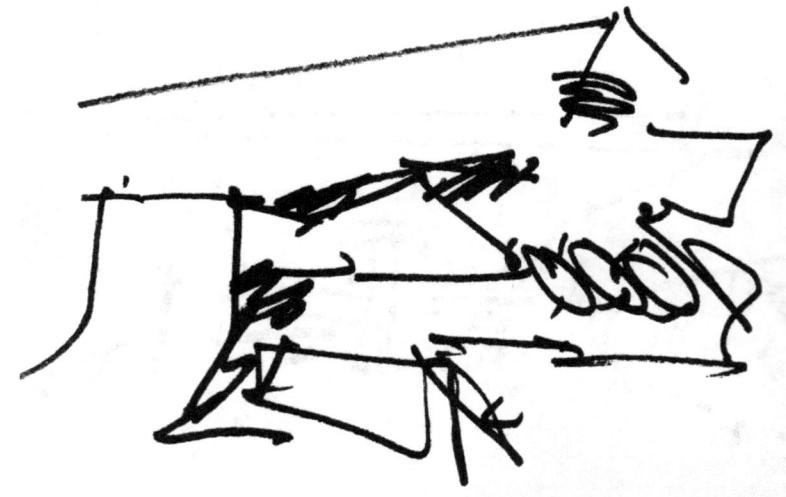

Efrain Recinos designed a brutalist / mayan theater for Guatemala.

November 18
Salvador

João Filgueiras Lima places 12 concrete petals in a circle to create an amazing chapel.

November 19
Ouro Branco 1977

Éolo Maia wraps a 18th century ruin with a metal envelope to rebuild a chapel.

November 20
São Paulo 1985

Lina Bo Bardi understood
São Paulo when she moved
to Bahia, bdesigning her
masterpiece - SESC Pompeia -
2 decades later.

November 21
São Paulo 1988

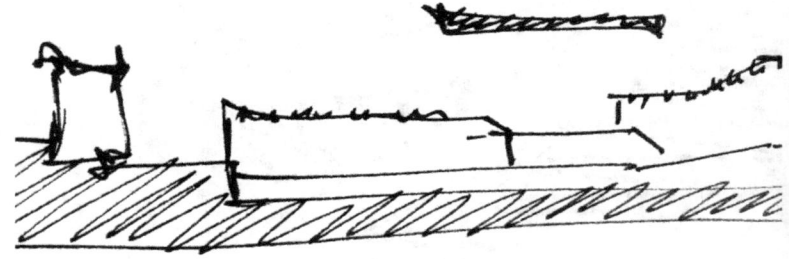

There was no collection but
Mendes da Rocha invented a
museum of sculpture our of
thin topography.

November 22
Brasilia 1991

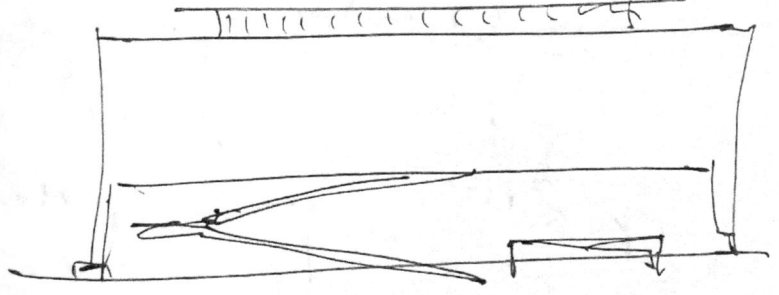

Paulo Mendes da Rocha chooses Bucci and Puntoni as his successors on the Sevillha Pavillion competition.

November 23
Buenos Aires 1993

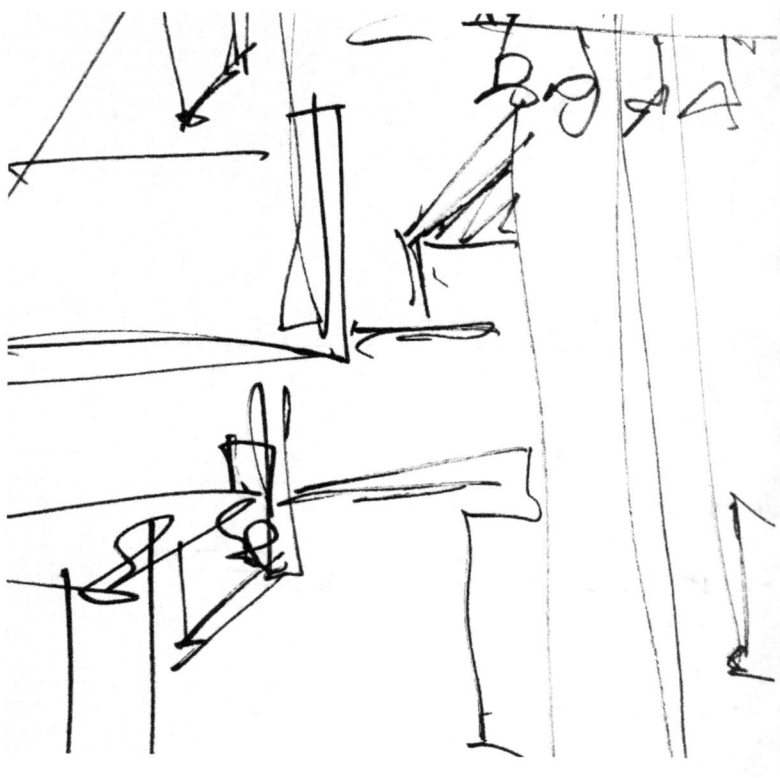

Pablo Beitia created the perfect spaces for Xul Solar watercolors.

November 24
Asunción

Solano Benitez built the most poetic homage to a father.

November 25
Rosario

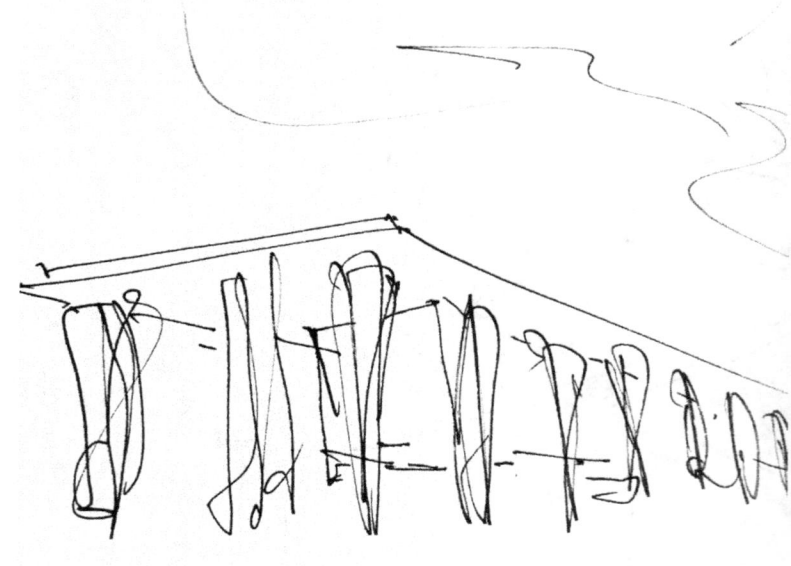

Rafael Iglesia mastery of materials serves the public of Parque Independencia.

November 26
Inhotim

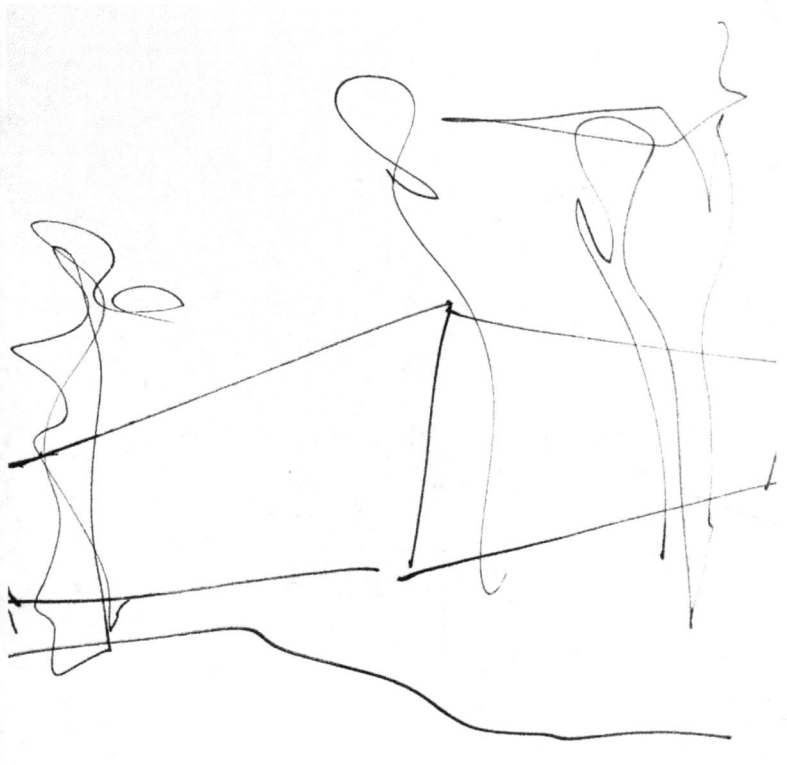

A corten steel box houses
a collection of hard cold
photographs.

November 27
El Cabuyal

Very young architects change
the word by building a school
with their own hands.

November 28
Cantinho do Céu

What if the garbage dump turns into the very best space in the community?

November 29
Concepcion

Formal geometry, when well done, can stir emotions too.

November 30
Medellin

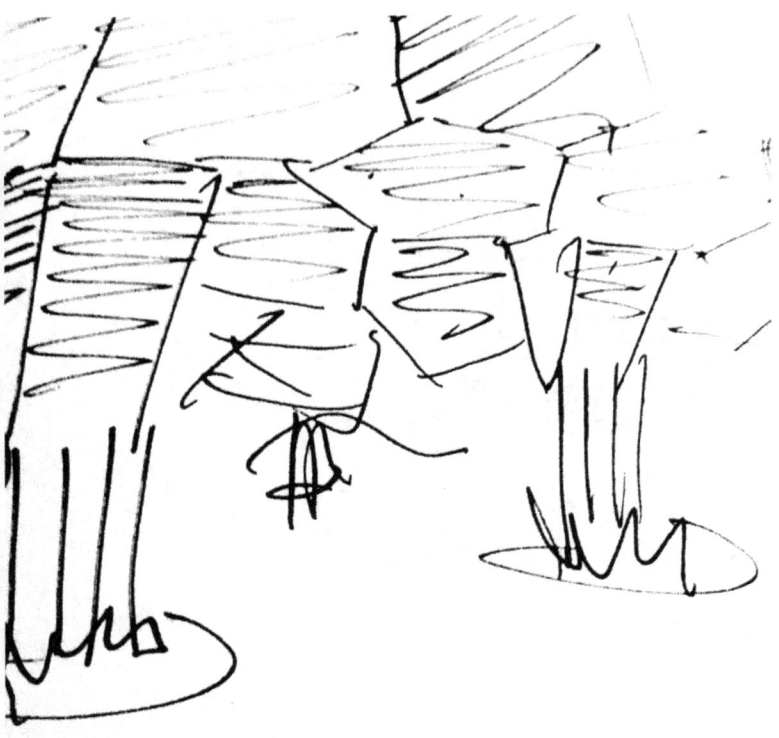

The most simple materials,
composed with a small rotation,
generates enough complexity
to awe.

December 01
Quito

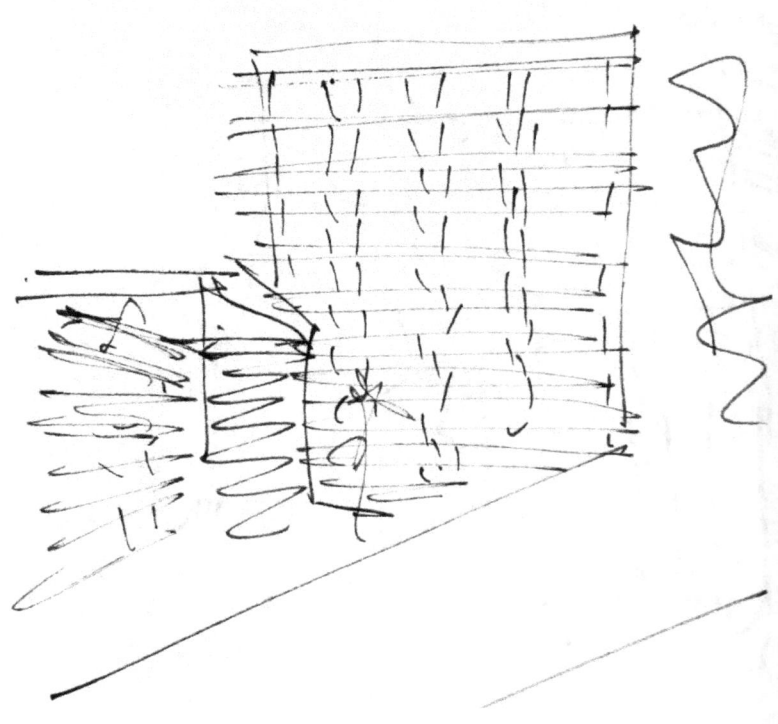

Where are the real architecture of the Americas? Quito government complex.

December 02
Vancouver

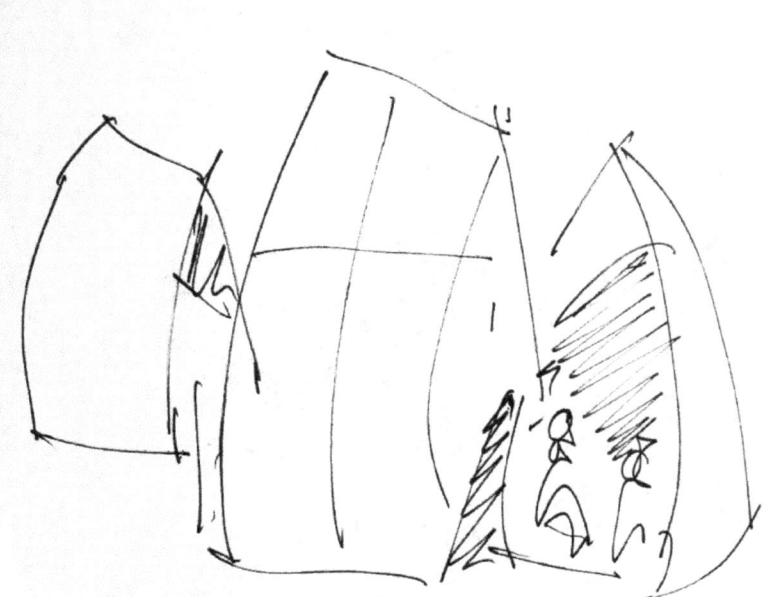

Patkau architects builds winter shelter by bending plywood.

December 03
Inhotim

It makes sense to name this building after Roberto Burle Marx for it does blend with the landscape.

December 04
El Alto

Freddy Mamani pushes the limits of our definition of architecture.

December 05
Ciudad de Mexico

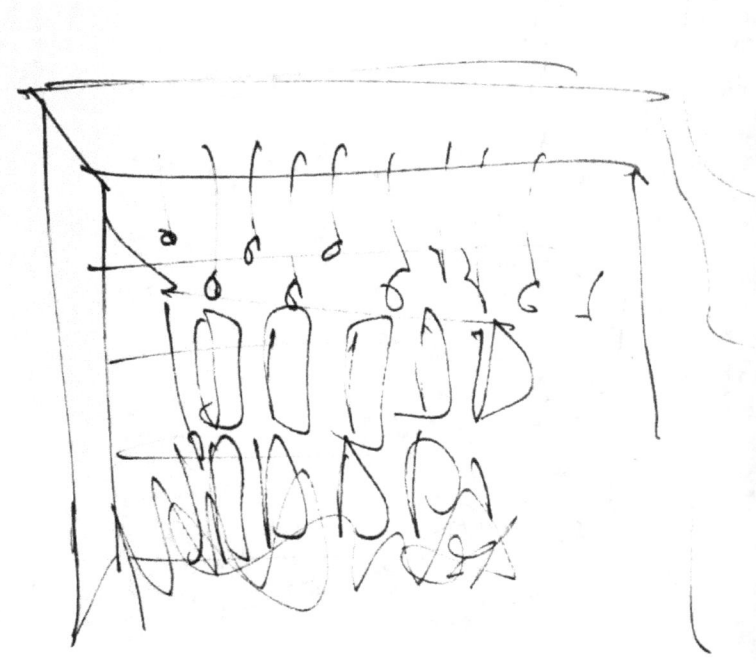

The old and the new should always shine together.

December 06
Asunción

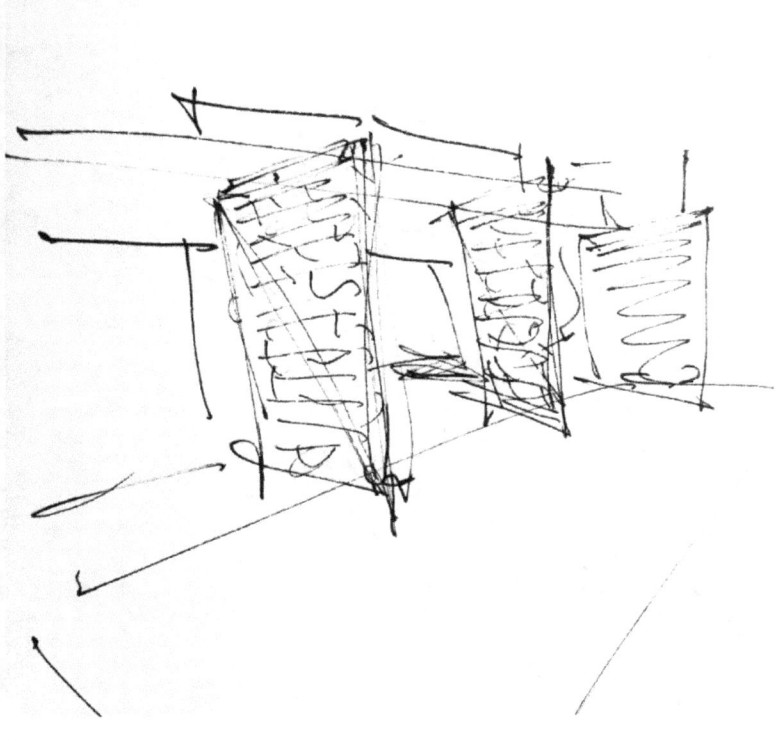

Joseto Cubilla opens the house to the breeze and the rain.

December 07
Quito

Ernesto Bilbao shows the future by turning an airport into a park.

December 08
Inhotim

Brazil is explained in the trail between Claudia Andujar and Miguel Rio Branco.

December 09
Rosario

Rafael Iglesia makes concrete float.

December 10
Jalisco

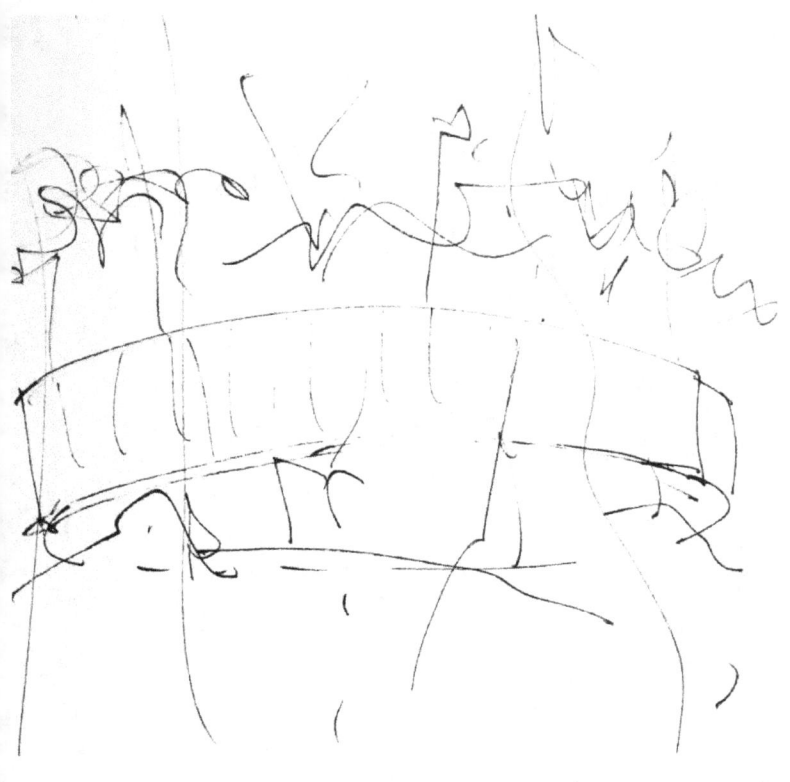

Derek Dellekamp builds the most poetic ring around the woods.

December 11
Talca

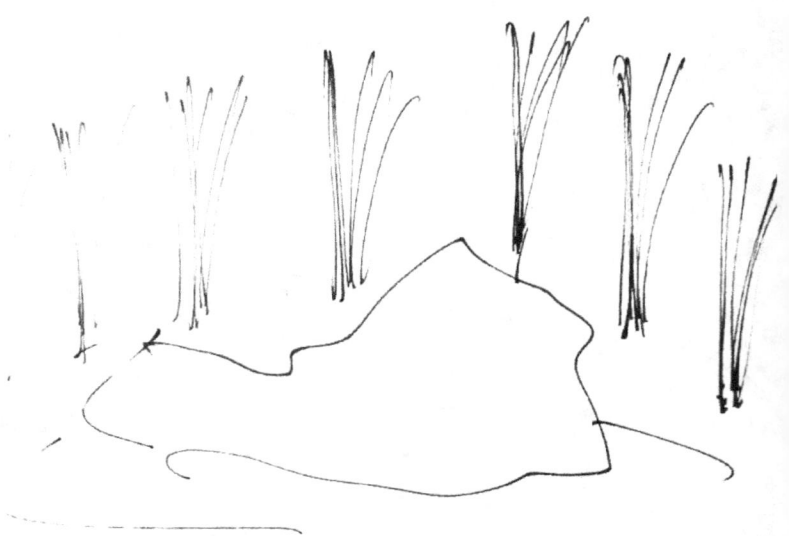

The future of design education
is already happening in Talca.

December 12
Santiago

Imagine building a 3-story office and leaving with the garbage/debris in a couple of bags.

December 13
Aldeia Xucuru

The Ema landing of Cacique Chicão challenge my spatial knowledge.

December 14
São Paulo

Marcos Boldarini proves that low income housing can and should look the best.

December 15
Caracas

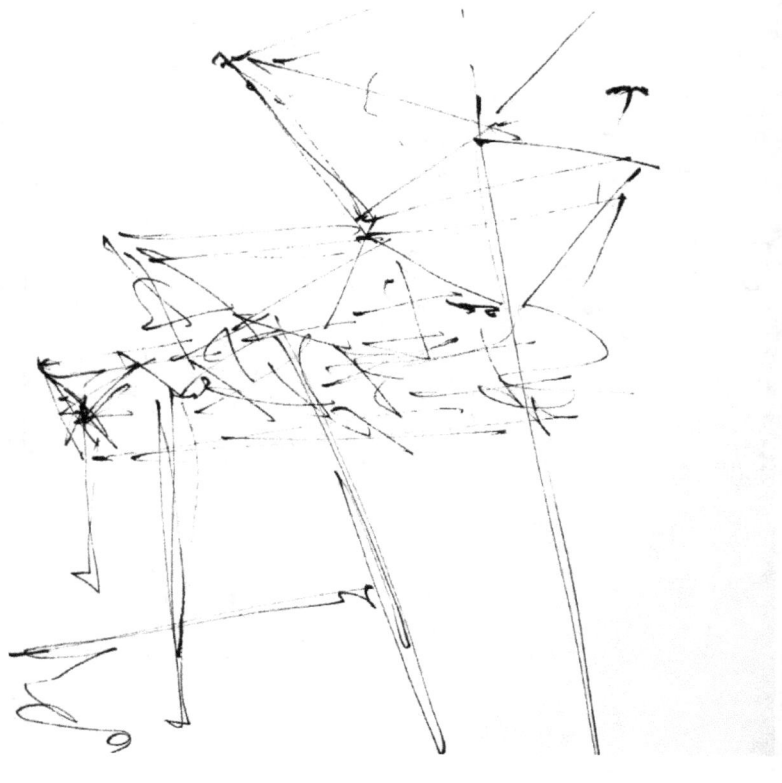

Espacios de Paz trusts that architecture can make a difference in the most difficult contexts.

December 16
Austin

Alejandro Araveña's student housing is the best building in town.

December 17
Queretaro

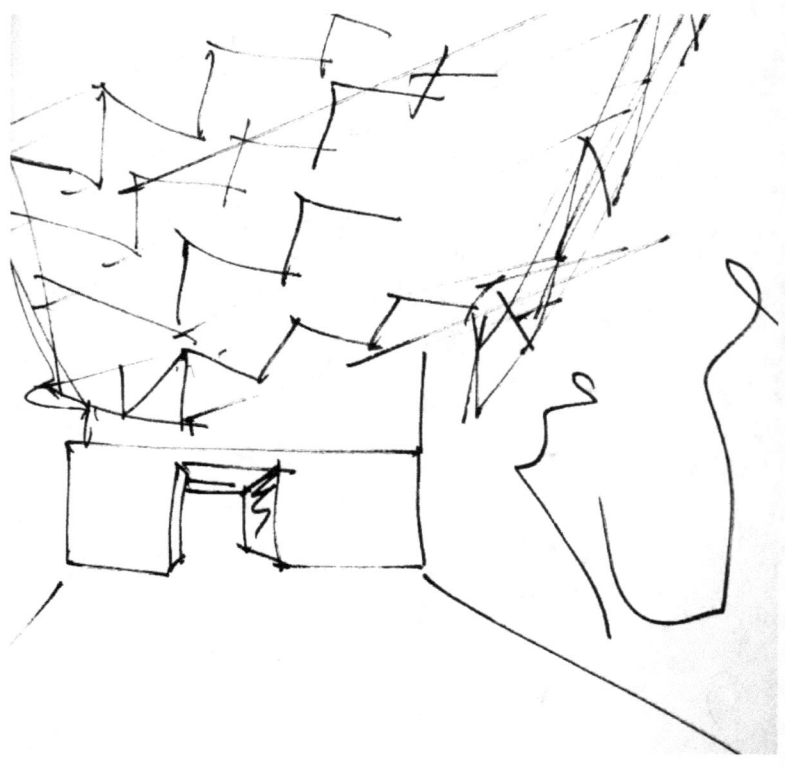

Poncho Garduño believes that architecture can deliver a better word.

December 18
Asuncion

Aqua Alta makes a difference with very little.

December 19
Rio de Janeiro

Carla Juaçaba builds a manifesto
with scaffolding.

December 20
Rio de Janeiro

Thaiago Bernardes stitches two buildings with a delicate canopy.

December 21
Santiago

Smiljan Radic highlights the strength of rocks.

December 22
Cuernavaca

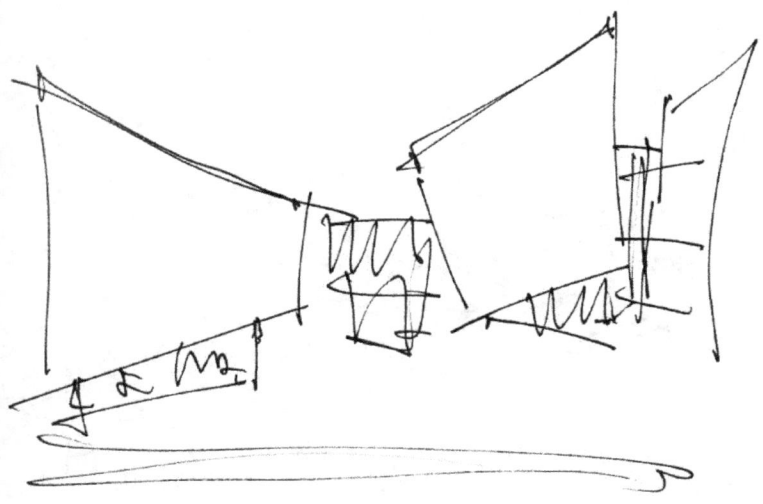

Frida Escobedo builds for Siqueros.

December 23
San Pedro

Sometimes the market is the community core.

December 24
Ciudad Acuña

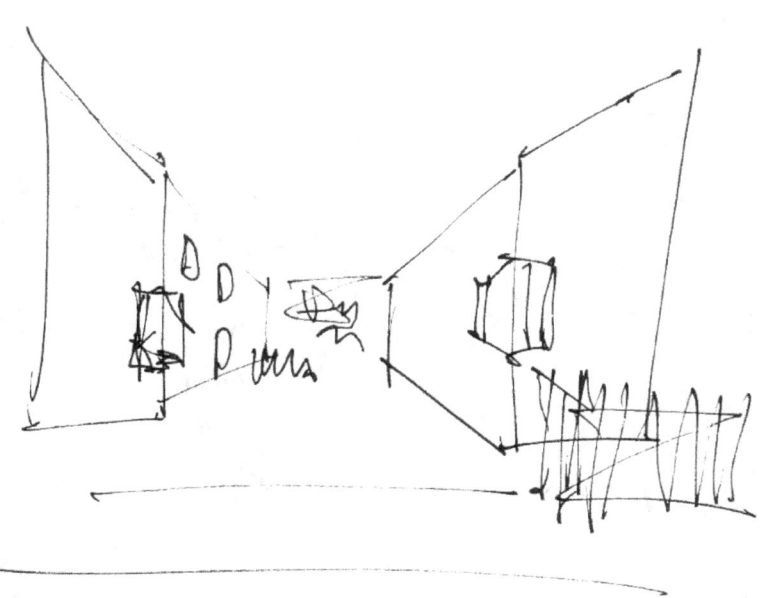

Tatiana Bilbao redesigns the simplest house.

December 25
Cretaús

Rede Arquitetos absorbs the sun as design element.

December 26
São Paulo

Andrade and
Moretin redefine
the architectural
components.

December 27
Jarinú

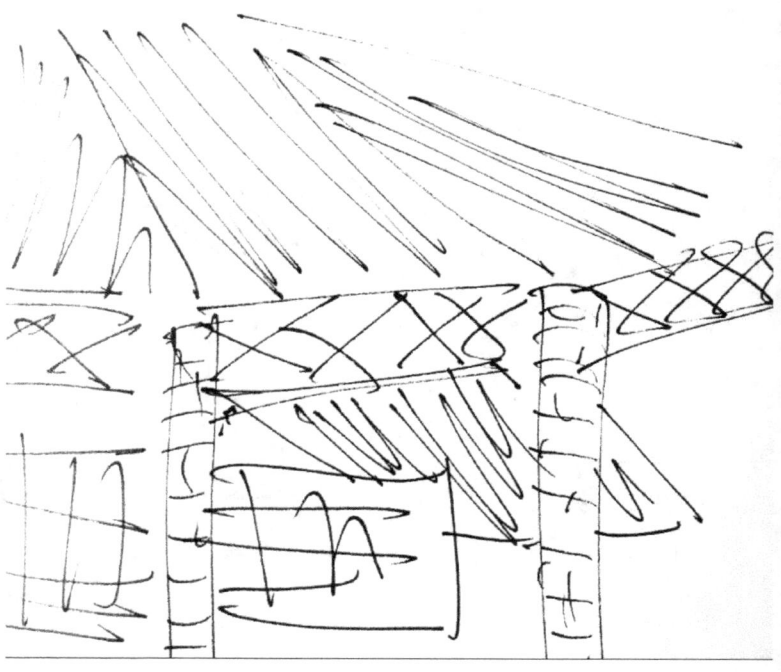

A palm tree in Tupi.

December 28
Grano de Oro

Kapaklajui indigenous center by Entre Nos in Costa Rica.

December 29
Paxixil

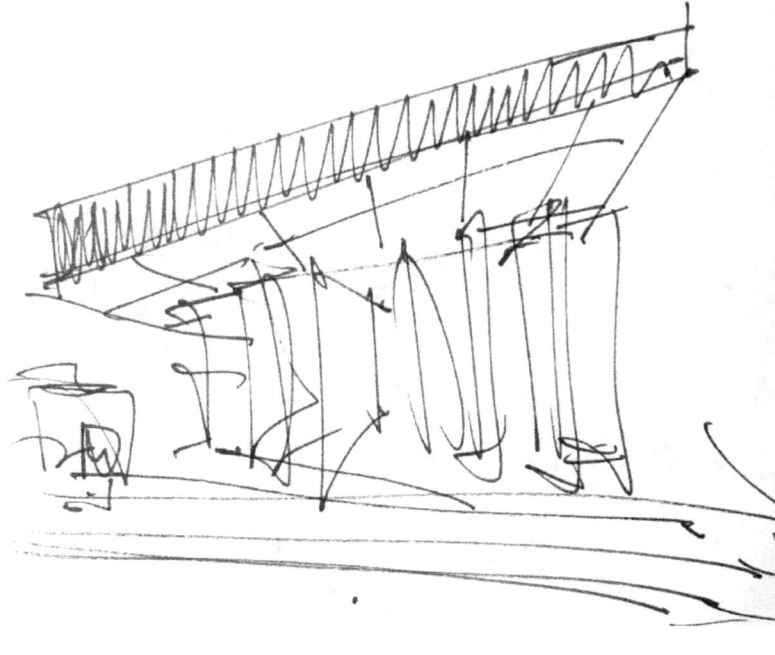

Axel Paredes turns a library into an indigenous force.

December 30
Ti Kay La

Small house in creole - Haiti.

December 31
Chinati

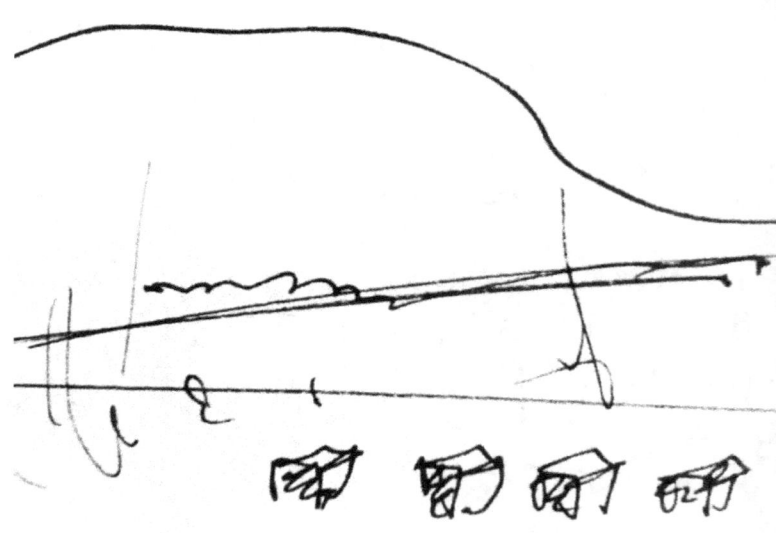

Donald Judd formalist utopia in the desert.